D0192595

MURDER & MYSTERY

MYSTERY

ON THE TITANIC

MURDER & MYSTERY

ON THE TITANIC

Mike Holgate

HALSGROVE

First published in Great Britain in 2011

Copyright © Mike Holgate 2011

All rights reserved. No part of this publication may be reproduced, stored in a retrieval system, or transmitted in any form or by any means without the prior permission of the copyright holder.

British Library Cataloguing-in-Publication Data
A CIP record for this title is available from the British Library

ISBN 978 0 85704 121 0

HALSGROVE
Halsgrove House,
Ryelands Business Park,
Bagley Road, Wellington, Somerset TA21 9PZ
Tel: 01823 653777   Fax: 01823 216796
email: sales@halsgrove.com

Part of the Halsgrove group of companies
Information on all Halsgrove titles is available at: www.halsgrove.com

Pri ... MPG Book Group

Newcastle Libraries & Information Service	
C4 666390 00 62	
Askews & Holts	Feb-2012
363.123	£12.99

CONTENTS

ACKNOWLEDGEMENTS

The author would like to extend his grateful thanks for material made available by Titanic devotée Scott Izard and Torbay Libraries for access to book, magazine, newspaper and online resources. Identifying suitable subjects for inclusion in the work was simplified by the availability of contemporary newspaper reports compiled by Dave Bryson (UK), and Eric Caren and Steve Goldman (USA), and the army of worldwide contributors to the gloriously named and highly informative website Encyclopedia-Titanica. Images obtained from Torbay Libraries were supplemented by the collections of the author and Scott Izard. The pictures selected were mainly published in contemporary journals and periodicals including: *The Daily Sketch, The Fallen Pillar, The Graphic, The Illustrated London News, Lloyd's Weekly News, New York Herald, The Sphere.*

INTRODUCTION
TRAGIC TALES OF THE TITANIC

*'I remember that it occurred to me that the good
God had stretched out His mighty hand and checked
further murder by His elements'. Arthur Rostron,
master of rescue ship* Carpathia

A century ago on 31 May 2011, the world's largest vessel was launched by the White Star Line in Belfast and proudly named the *Titanic*. Within a year, inquiries were held on both sides of the Atlantic counting the cost of an unthinkable tragedy that had befallen an 'unsinkable' vessel. Contemporary newspaper opinions that the needless loss of so many lives was a 'crime' or 'murder'

were ignored as the ship's owners did not even face charges of manslaughter or gross negligence. The mysterious disaster that occurred either side of midnight on the 14 and 15 April 1912, was succinctly summarised by the editor of the London weekly newspaper *Penny Illustrated*: 'A calm clear night, a huge ship ploughing along through it on a track as familiar as the Canterbury road to the pilgrims of old; men and women at cards, asleep, or at work; a bump, a hurried order to get the women into the boats, some panic, some shooting, and then fifteen hundred souls in the sea and seven hundred on it'.

As a writer specialising in unsolved mysteries and true-life crime, it was intriguing to read eye-witness accounts that armed ship's officers, opened fire and allegedly killed male passengers they were supposedly trying to save, whenever the policy of 'women and children first' was threatened. My interest was further stimulated upon learning that Robert Hichens, the helmsman at the moment of impact with the iceberg, was arrested some twenty years later for an attempted murder committed in my home town. From this starting point, it was possible to unearth a murky mixture of murder, mystery and myth with two convicted killers amongst the crew, several other members who suffered multiple shipwrecks, horrific experiences in the ensuing world war, ten survivors whose tragic lives later drove them to commit suicide and numerous instances where people experienced omens that, like Nostradamus, predicted the world's greatest maritime tragedy. A presentiment of disaster foreseen by band leader Wallace Hartley was shared by journalist, spiritualist and convicted child abductor, William Stead. According to a medium, the latter revealed from beyond the grave that it was he who asked the ship's musicians to perform the poignant hymn 'Nearer My God To Thee'.

Mike Holgate
Torquay, 31 May 2011

MYSTERY AND CRIME ON THE WHITE STAR LINE

HEROES AND VILLAINS

On the tenth day of April
Nineteen hundred and twelve,
A new ship named the *Titanic*
Sailed from England bound for Hell.

On board the ill-fated vessel
Were men from all walks of life,
Heroes and villains
Doomed to die side by side.

The millionaire paid with his life
No matter how revered his name,
The fugitive had nowhere to hide
On the ship that died of shame.

When the stricken ship was sinking
Men panicked fearing the worst,
Shots rang out to uphold the law
Of 'women and children first'.

Mike Holgate

WILLIAM MURDOCH
'WOMEN AND CHILDREN FIRST'

'I saw Mr Murdoch shoot down an Italian'

When the so-called 'unsinkable' *Titanic* struck an iceberg and began to founder on her maiden voyage from Southampton to New York in April 1912, the ship's captain, Edward Smith, issued firearms to his officers. Fearing there may be trouble, they were prepared to prevent a rush for the insufficient number of lifeboats (intended to carry 1200) that subsequently carried only 705 of the 2,340 passengers and crew to safety. As the death toll rose to an appalling total of 1,595, praise was given to the lack of panic displayed by male passengers who met their deaths having admirably observed the ancient rule of the sea, 'women and children first'. Held back at gunpoint, most of the 'heroic' men stoically kissed their wives goodbye and helplessly stood by watching half-empty lifeboats carrying people away from the doomed vessel. A total of only twenty-two passengers were called to the subsequent inquiries into the tragedy held in New York and London. From members of the crew, detailed evidence of one shooting incident was heard, where Fifth Officer Harold Lowe fired his revolver several times along the side of the stricken ship to warn off some steerage passengers who were attempting to jump into a lifeboat. Many stories of actual killings that had emerged in the press were seemingly not investigated, including a statement purportedly released by a committee of survivors who claimed that 'three Italians were shot to death in the struggle for the lifeboats'.

Most men stoically kissed their wives goodbye and stood by watching while half-empty lifeboats were launched.

Among the first survivors to embark from the rescue ship *Carpathia* in New York was Washington Dodge who was saved along with his wife and their three-year-old son. Surrounded by reporters, he described the final torrid scenes on the *Titanic*, 'Good order prevailed at first. Later, when everyone realised that the ship was sinking, the men became as wild as the women. After we had gone over with the lifeboat, I heard as many as fifty shots fired, which was evidence to me that there had been scenes of dreadful fighting aboard'. Californian George Brayton gave more damning evidence to the press, stating how he saw a foreigner shot down as he tried to press past a number of women in order to gain a place in the lifeboats. An unnamed passenger praised the gunman and identified him as the ill-fated First Officer William Murdoch: 'I saw Mr Murdoch shoot down an Italian. This officer performed heroic work all through'.

A dramatic tale was told by Ellen Shine, a twenty-year-old girl from County Cork, Ireland, who was among a group of women from the steerage who rushed to the upper decks and pushed their way past members of the crew and made for the lifeboats. 'I saw a lifeboat and jumped into it', Miss Shine told reporters, 'In it were four men from steerage. They were ordered out by an officer and refused to leave. And then one of the officers jumped into the lifeboat and, drawing a revolver, shot the four men dead. Their bodies were picked out from the bottom of the boat and thrown into the ocean'.

Although syndicated newspaper reports alleging that passengers were shot down in cold blood may be attributed to hysterical rumours or press sensationalism, it does not explain why eyewitness accounts were relayed in letters immediately sent by survivors to their families. Two men separately alleged that an unnamed officer (widely reported in the press to be William Murdoch whose body was never found) perpetrated the killings then proceeded to shoot himself. Steerage passenger, Eugene Daly, wrote a graphic account to his sister in Ireland: 'When a boat was

William Murdoch allegedly shot passengers then himself.

being lowered, an officer pointed a revolver and said if any man tried to get in he would shoot him on the spot. I saw the officer shoot two men dead because they tried to get into the boat. Afterwards there was another shot, and I saw the officer himself lying on the deck. They told me he shot himself, but I did not see him. I was up to my knees in water at the time. Everyone was rushing around and there were no more boats. I then dived overboard and got in a boat'.

First Class passenger George Rheims' description of the same incident, varied only slightly in the number of casualties involved. In a letter to his wife in France, written the day after arriving in New York, he unwittingly confirmed Daly's observations: 'While the last boat was leaving, I saw an officer with a revolver fire a shot and kill a man who was trying to climb into it. As there remained nothing more for him to do, the officer told us, "Gentlemen, each man for himself. Goodbye". He gave a military salute and then fired a bullet into his head. That's what I call a man!!!'

ROBERT HICHENS
SINKING LOWER AND LOWER

'I shan't give the hangman a job'

Quartermaster Robert Hichens was the helmsman at the wheel of the *Titanic* at the moment of impact with the iceberg. Put in charge of a lifeboat, Hichens was criticised at the subsequent inquiry held in New York, for swigging whisky and ignoring pleas from other occupants of the boat to search the water for survivors, 'No, we are not going back to the boat', he said curtly, 'It is our lives now, not theirs'. As the ship disappeared beneath the waves, the cries and

screams of people fighting for their lives in the water was plainly heard in the still night air, Hichens cruelly summed up the situation, 'It's no use; there's only a lot of stiffs out there'.

The inhumane attitude and over-reliance on drink displayed by Hichens at this great moment of crisis was to re-emerge some

Hichens warned: 'It is our lives now, not theirs'.

twenty years later in Torquay, the seaside resort known as 'The Queen of the English Riviera' where he failed disastrously to make a living running pleasure boat trips. It was in the same town, during the summer of 1906, that he had met his future wife, Florence Mortimore. She was visiting relatives, while he was on shore leave with the crew of a private yacht. Following a whirlwind courtship, the couple were married within a few months in the bride's home village of Manaton on Dartmoor. Settling firstly in Torquay, where the first two of their six children were born, then Southampton, Hichens secured a prestigious appointment on the newly launched luxury liner *Titanic*. Following the terrible maritime disaster, he returned to sea, served with the naval reserve during the First World War, then spent some time working as a harbourmaster in South Africa. By 1930, he was back in Torquay as owner of the *Princess Elizabeth* pleasure boat, purchased from businessman Harry Henley, for which he made a down payment with the remainder to be paid within two years. The venture failed disastrously and he was unable to repay the balance. Furthermore, Hichens had also borrowed the deposit from a Mr Squires who seized the boat to settle the debt following a poor season's trading in 1931. The loss of his business caused Hichens to turn to drink and by the end of that year his wife had left him and moved back to Southampton. Her troubled husband scoured the country unable to find work and unreasonably chose to lay the blame for his predicament on the man who had sold him the boat. On his travels he acquired a revolver and journeyed back to Torquay determined to kill Harry Henley. Upon his arrival in November 1933, he looked up an old friend of twenty years standing, fisherman Thomas Holden and told him, 'There will be two less in Torquay tonight. I've come down to do Henley and myself.' By early evening Hichens was drinking with another acquaintance, docker Joe Stroud, who hearing of the plan and shown the revolver warned, 'Put it away. Don't be a fool. He isn't worth swinging for'. Worse the wear for drink the gunman appeared to see sense and replied, 'I'll take your tip, I shan't give the

Robert Hichens giving evidence at the inquiry in London.

hangman a job'. However, after closing time, having consumed rum in at least three public houses during the course of the evening, Hichens took a taxi and alighted outside the home of Harry Henley.

Hearing a knock at the door, Henley came outside to see Hichens standing with both hands in his trouser pockets. 'Do you remember me Harry? slurred the inebriated Hichens. 'Why of course I do' replied Henley. 'What do you want?' The unexpected caller demanded more money, to which, his creditor replied, 'I wouldn't give you a penny piece if you were lying in the gutter'. Hichens then pulled out the pistol and with the words 'Take that' raised the weapon to the level of his target's head. Two shots were fired and Hichens very nearly succeeded in his desire to kill his former business associate. The first bullet grazed the side of the victim's head. Henley felt a searing pain and subsequently lost a lot of blood but was fortunate not to suffer serious injury. The second shot went downwards and wide as Henley pushed Hichens away and punched his assailant in the face giving him a bloody nose. Hichens fell to floor giving Henley the opportunity to run away and summon the police. Meanwhile, the gunman got up and staggered thirty yards before laying down on the footpath where he tentatively put the revolver to his head and pulled the trigger, but the bullet passed harmlessly by. Taken to the police station in an intoxicated state, Hichens enquired, 'Is he dead? I hope he is. He is a dirty rat, I would do it again if I had a chance, I intended to kill him and myself, too. He has taken my living away.'

Brought to trial for attempted murder, the prisoner received a sympathetic hearing from the judge after appearing with dressings on his wrists as he had made a desperate attempt to slash his wrists while held in custody. The defendant's previous good character and the fact that he appeared to be a 'broken man' influenced the lenient outcome of five years' imprisonment. Despite the murderous attack having been fermenting in Hichens' mind for many months, his defence counsel successfully contended that the incident had been precipitated only because his client was under the influence of alcohol. With an unintended pun, the lawyer explained that since the terrible ordeal on the *Titanic* his client had been 'sinking lower and lower'.

WILLIAM MINTRAM
REDEMPTION OF A WIFE KILLER

'Wake up... we've hit an iceberg'

Fate played a hand when convicted killer William Mintram was paroled for 'good behaviour' and released from prison in time to resume his career at sea, stoking the coal furnaces on the *Titanic*. Had he completed the full term, the prisoner would have escaped the death sentence that awaited him – a fate he had narrowly avoided for occasioning the death of a defenceless woman ten years earlier.

Living in Southampton, mariner William Mintram wed Eliza Veal in 1886 and the couple raised five children. The Mintrams' marriage came to a violent end soon after their fifteenth wedding anniversary. Having visited a public house until late in the evening, the drunken husband returned to the marital home. His wife had prepared his supper but was much the worse for wear herself, having consumed an amount of 'mother's ruin'. When her drunken spouse discovered that she had obtained money for gin by pawning the shoes of their twelve-year-old son, William junior, a quarrel broke out. The row subsided briefly when a policeman warned the warring couple about their behaviour, then dispersed a crowd that had gathered outside the property. Half-an-hour later the dispute erupted again with fatal consequences. The only witness to the incident was the young barefooted William, who saw his father slap his mother across the face as she sat in a chair. The assaulted woman retaliated and rushed at her attacker who grabbed a kitchen knife and stabbed

Lord Mersey was the judge at Mintrams' trial.

her once in the back. Taken to hospital, the victim was pronounced dead on arrival. Arrested and tried for wilful murder before Mr Justice Bigham (who later, as Lord Mersey, would conduct the *Titanic* Inquiry as President of the Wreck Commissioner's Court), William Mintram admitted he was intoxicated and remembered little of the affair, apart from the fact that he had been nagged by his wife. Five children, aged between five and fifteen, seemed certain to become orphans as the prisoner faced the prospect of execution for his crime. However, after hearing about the turbulent state of the Mintrams' marriage and the previous excellent character of the thirty-three-year-old defendant – who had supported a large family by toiling at sea as a fireman for many years – the jury showed mercy and found the accused not culpable for murder, but guilty of manslaughter. The trial judge imposed a sentence of twelve years' imprisonment in November 1902, but by 1912, Mintram had been granted a 'ticket of leave' and was residing in Southampton next door to his eldest child Rosina, who was now a mother. Her husband of five years Walter 'Wally' Hurst and his father, Charles, were seamen with the White Star Line. Mintram joined his two relatives in signing on as stoker aboard the newly-launched pride of the fleet, a voyage from which only one of the trio would return alive.

When tragedy struck the vessel, Charles Hurst was on duty in the stokehold. He rushed to warn his off-watch son and threw a lump of ice on to his bunk shouting: 'Wake up, Wally, we've hit an iceberg'. Discovering that his son-in-law did not a have a lifejacket,

Wally Hurst leapt sevety-five feet into the water.

William Mintram partially redeemed himself for his past sins by selflessly handing him his own. Making his way to the boat deck, Wally jumped into the sea from a height of seventy-five feet, only five minutes before the ship sank. Upon his safe return to England, he told the press that, having been immersed in the ocean for over three hours, he could not have lasted much longer. Luckily, he was fished out of the water by the occupants of a lifeboat. Later informed that his father and father-in-law had perished and only six men among the ten engineers, five leading firemen, ten greasers, twenty-five trimmers, and fifty-three firemen on duty in the engine room and stokehold had survived, he paid a fitting tribute to his fallen comrades: 'My mates', he said, 'received orders to remain below and rake out the fires to prevent explosions. They obeyed them at the sacrifice of their lives'.

MICHEL NAVRATIL
ORPHANS OF THE TITANIC

'Mamma is in Nice'

When Michel Navratil was beset with financial worries and marital problems he made a decision that would cost him his life and inadvertently spark off an international mystery. The Hungarian tailor had moved to France and settled in Nice, with his Buenos Aires wife of Italian extraction, Marcello, whom he had married in London. But after five years of wedlock, Michel's business was failing and his marriage broke down when he suspected his wife was having an affair. The couple separated and while divorce proceedings were pending, Michel sold his shop and made a plan to flee the country and start a new life in America with his two young sons, Edmond and Michel junior, aged two and nearly four respectively. When their mother allowed the children to stay with their father over the Easter period in 1912, Michel Navratil immediately absconded and, travelling in the name of a family friend, Louis Hoffman, took the boys via Monte Carlo to London and purchased second class tickets on the *Titanic*, boarding at Southampton.

When disaster struck, 'Mr Hoffman', observed the rule of 'women and children first' and allowed his sons to be placed alone in a lifeboat leaving the sinking ship. Many years later Michel junior recalled that his father must have realised he was facing certain death, when he gave him a final message, 'My child, when your mother comes for you, as she surely will, tell her that I loved her dearly and still do. Tell her I expected her to follow us, so that we might all live happily together in the peace and freedom of the New World'. His father's body was recovered floating in a life jacket and among the items found on his person was a revolver – raising the possibility that he had intended to use it on the boys and himself if apprehended by the law. Fellow passengers had been led to believe that the children's mother was dead, so, as the boys were cared for at the New York home of first class survivor Margaret Hays, a world-wide search was launched to find relatives of the boys known by their assumed names, 'Louis' and 'Lolo' whom the press dubbed the 'waifs of the sea' and 'orphans of the *Titanic*'.

Their frantic mother, Marcello Navratil, read newspaper reports about the plight of the boys. It confirmed her suspicions that her husband had travelled on the *Titanic* as he had often expressed a desire to emigrate to America. Positive identification of her two 'kidnapped' sons was soon made possible when she described some

slight scars on the body of the younger child 'Lolo'. 'Foster-mother' Margaret Hays announced that, 'There is no longer any doubt that Mme. Navratil is the mother of the children... We kept the existence of the marks a secret for just this purpose, knowing that if a parent could describe them identification

The abducted 'orphans' reunited with their mother.

would be positive'. Miss Hays received further confirmation when she casually spoke to the boys in their native tongue roughly translated as, 'What do you know about Nice?' to which they replied, 'Mamma is in Nice'.

The White Star Line arranged for Mme. Navratil to be reunited with her children by booking a passage on the *Oceanic*. At a conference with 'la presse' in New York, the pretty twenty-one-year-old widow explained to reporters that following the birth of their two children her late husband's jealous behaviour had become 'unreasonable' and the couple agreed to separate. A reconciliation lasted only three days before Easter when she had seen her husband for the last time on Good Friday. When the single-parent was asked whether she would consider any of the many offers of adoption, she held the children tight to her and dismissed the foolish query, 'No, indeed. I couldn't give them up,' adding that she had no fears about the future or her ability to provide adequately for the boys from her earnings as a sales assistant in a department store. Despite his ordeal, little Michel was dressed in a sailor suit and his favourite toy was a model boat. His mother revealed that he still had no fear of the sea, although she was worried how he might react on the journey back home as he had been terrified of aircraft since seeing someone killed at an air show in Nice.

Once repatriated in their homeland, Edmond Navratil grew up to become an architect and fought with the French Army in the Second World War. Held as a prisoner-of-war after being captured, he escaped from the camp where conditions had severely effected his health from which he never fully recovered. He died at the age of forty-three in 1951. In contrast, his elder brother, Michel lived to become the oldest male survivor of the *Titanic*. In 2001, the professor of psychology died at the age of ninety-two. Late in life, he crossed the Atlantic for the first time since 1912 to visit the grave of his father in Halifax, Nova Scotia. During the trip, he also spent time in New York, six months prior to the 75th anniversary of the maritime tragedy in 1997.

GEORGE McGOUGH
MANSLAUGHTER ON THE HIGH SEAS

'I have done it like a man and I will swing like a man'

Newly-wed able seaman George McGough, who manned one of the *Titanic's* lifeboats, visited the Catholic Seaman's Mission in New York and revealed that two priests had spent their last hours consoling and taking confessions of immigrants in the third class steerage before they went down, with the ship. According to McGough, the churchmen had boarded the *Titanic* in Ireland and were not on the official passenger list. McGough also took the opportunity to complain to the press that officials of the White Star Line in New York had refused to allow him and other surviving crew members of the doomed ship to go ashore. In his opinion the seamen had been treated like 'prisoners' – ironically, a situation that he had experienced previously when it was alleged that he 'feloniously, wilfully and of malice aforethought, did kill and murder' shipmate John Dwyer by attacking and throwing him down the hold of the steamer *Rustington*, while she was lying in the harbour of Santos, Brazil in March 1900.

The *Rustington* had delivered a cargo of coal after sailing from Cardiff six weeks earlier. Among the crew were two men fated to meet in mortal combat, George McGough and John Dwyer, a well-liked boarding house keeper from Barry. Having spent several weeks at sea, the crew went ashore in Santos and returned to the

McGough manned one of the Titanic's *lifeboats.*

ship shortly before ten o'clock in the evening. All had been drinking but McGough was particularly intoxicated. Spoiling for a fight, he challenged any of his companions to take him on. Dwyer tried to pacify McGough, but the belligerent Irishman from Duncannon would not be persuaded to go below and sleep it off. The two seamen engaged in a scuffle before McGough suddenly rushed at Dwyer, butted him in the stomach, then grabbed his legs and upended him down the open hatchway of the hold. The victim of the unprovoked assault fell a distance of over twenty feet and landed on his head. Blood poured from his ears, nose and mouth and he died from his injuries within minutes. Four members of the crew witnessed the attack and McGough was clapped in irons. Handed over to the British Consul in Santos, the prisoner was brought back to England on board the Royal Mail steamship *Magdelena*. When the ship put into her home port at Southampton, the accused killer was formally arrested by the police and, after a magistrate's hearing, was sent for trial at Hampshire Summer Assizes held at Winchester before Mr Justice Lawrence.

The jury heard how the thirty-nine-year-old deceased man, who left a widow and seven children, had been reluctant to fight and tried in vain to defend himself against the quarrelsome prisoner. One of the witnesses was John Dwyer's brother-in-law, William Burnett, a donkey man on the *Rustington*. He testified that following the tragedy, he and other members of the crew went down into the hold where they found the badly haemorrhaging man close to death. When the men came back up on deck, the assailant remonstrated with them, 'Why don't you have that man up and go for a doctor, or shall I go for a doctor myself?'. Evidence was also heard from the ship's carpenter who recalled that when McGough was informed that it was too late to summon medical assistance and he would have to face his punishment for what he had done, the prisoner threatened to throw him down the hold as well unless he 'shut up'. In defence of the actions of the accused, his lawyer stated that it had all been a terrible accident. Death, he claimed had been caused by what would nowadays be described as a health and safety issue. He argued that John Dwyer would still be alive if the hatch had not carelessly been left open. Surprisingly, the judge agreed with this point of view and instructed the jury that there was no case of murder to be answered. Therefore, the defendant was found 'guilty' only of 'manslaughter on the high seas' and served a lenient sentence of fifteen months imprisonment with hard labour. The twenty-four-year-old prisoner was fortunate to escape the death penalty, for when first told that his victim was dead, he boasted, 'I have done it like a man and I will swing like a man'.

JAY YATES
GAMBLING WITH HIS LIFE

'I spent nearly a fortune getting him out of trouble
some years ago'

There was speculation in the American press that some of the doomed passengers on the *Titanic* were members of gangs of cardsharps and conmen preying on rich men for 'easy pickings'. Among the crooks thought to be plying their trade on 'The Great White Way,' travelling under assumed names, were: 'Doc' Owen, 'Old Man' Jordan, 'One Arm Mac', Jim Kitchener, Tom McAuliffe, William Day, Peaches Van Camp, Buffalo Murphy, James Gordon and Frankie Dwyer.

According to the New York correspondent of the *Chicago Inter-Ocean* newspaper they were 'a flock of buzzards of the sea, human vampires who preyed on the passengers crossing the Atlantic... Reports reached here that some of them got away in the lifeboats, and it is an even bet on Broadway that if there was a chance "for a minute" more than one got into the boats as a sailor or as a shrieking woman in distress'.

Apparently, such cowardly conduct was not displayed by conman and fugitive from justice Jay Yates. Travelling on the liner using the alias J. M. Rogers, he reportedly went down with the *Titanic* after helping women and children into the lifeboats. Before plunging into the sea where he drowned, he handed a lady a note written on a blank page torn from a diary: 'If [you are] saved, inform my sister, Mrs. J. F. Adams of Findlay, Ohio. Lost. [Signed] J. H.

The lifeboat gamble with Death.

Rogers.' The woman then anonymously enlisted the help of the press to deliver the bad news to the dead man's family:

> You will find note that was handed to me as I was leaving the *Titanic*. Am stranger to this man but think he was a card player. He helped me aboard a lifeboat and I saw him help others. Before we were lowered I saw him jump into the sea. If picked up I did not see him on the *Carpathia*. I do not think he was registered on the ship under his right name.

The gambler's mother Mary Yates broke down when told her son had perished: 'Thank God, I know where he is now,' she sobbed. 'I have not heard from him for two years. The last news I had from him he was in London. I spent nearly a fortune getting him out of trouble some years ago. Then he was charged with forgery.' However, the criminal's untimely end may have been yet another con-trick. At the time of the *Titanic* sinking, he was on the run for the theft of $2,700 in postal money orders that he had persuaded an unsuspecting cousin to cash for him. A string of further offences were committed in Cincinnati, Chicago, Indiana-polis, St Louis, Los Angeles, San Francisco and Boston. It is probable that the note about his presence on the ill-fated ship was a ruse to put the police off the scent, as in June 1912, an unsubstanti-ated report claimed that the supposed victim of drown-ing was arrested in Baltimore using the name Albert Berger.

Legendary gambler 'Titanic' Thompson.

The aftermath of the *Titanic* tragedy also created a legendary gambler and hustler who became the inspiration for the character Sky Masterson in Damon Runyon's story 'Guys and Dolls'. Alvin Clarence Thomas known as '*Titanic*' Thompson had a lucrative career wagering at cards and dice games. He was also a multi-talented sportsman who used his skills at pool and golf to win bets. One favourite hustle was to beat a golfer playing right-handed, then offer double or nothing to play the course again left-handed as an apparent concession. The duped opponents were blissfully unaware that 'Titanic' was in fact, naturally left-handed. Looking back on his extraordinary life during an interview in 1972, the gambling genius explained how he had earned his unusual nickname sixty years earlier during his days as a pool shark:

> In the spring of 1912 I went to Joplin, Missouri, just about the time the [*Titanic*] liner hit an iceberg and sank with more than 1,500 people on board. I was in a pool room there and beat a fellow named Snow Clark out of $500. To give him a chance to get even, I bet $500 I could jump across his pool table without touching it. If you think that's easy try it. But I could jump farther than a herd of bullfrogs in those days. I put down an old mattress on the other side of the table. Then I took a run and dived headfirst across the pool table. When I was counting my money, somebody asked Clark what my name was, 'It must be *Titanic*', said Clark. 'He sinks everybody'. So I was *Titanic* from then on.

CHARLES BARNES
DOUBLE TROUBLE

'From your loving son, Robert Barnhouse'

For various reasons, some people travelled incognito on the *Titanic*. Although they were well-known society figures, Sir Cosmo and Lady Duff booked their passage as Mr and Mrs Morgan, while unmarried couple George Rosenshine and Maybelle Thorne kept up appearances listed as Mr and Mrs Thorne. Cardsharps George 'Boy' Bradley and Harry 'Kid' Homer assumed the names of George Brayton and E. Haven respectively. A year after the tragedy, in April 1913, at a hearing at Torquay County Court in Devon, the true identity of a stoker, who had died a year earlier on the *Titanic*, was established when a pensioner brought an action for compensation against the White Star Line, who had turned down an application in respect of his late son Robert Barnhouse, known by the alias Charles Barnes.

During the hearing, it emerged that Robert Barnhouse had been born at Barnstaple in 1870. The fifth of eight children, he had left his parents' home over twenty years before his death and became estranged from his family. He drifted to Bristol where his hands were badly burned in a fire at a licensed house run by William and Edith Curtis. Homeless and destitute, Barnhouse was taken in by the Curtis family to recuperate and remained with them until his untimely end. When William Curtis moved to Southampton to run a bakery, Barnhouse went too, and now, known as Charles Barnes, became a seaman. A chance meeting with his younger brother

Arthur, who worked as a railway cleaner at Eastleigh, near Southampton, re-established contact with his family in 1908. Their parents, George and Susan, had remained in Barnstaple until retirement age, then moved across the county to Torquay where one of their daughters, Elizabeth, lived with her husband, fish hawker, Joseph Moss. While serving on a vessel, 'Charles' obtained shore leave while the ship was in Plymouth and, accompanied by his brother Arthur, stayed with his parents at their new home in October 1911. Shortly afterwards the forty-one-year-old seaman transferred to the newly launched *Titanic* and was one of the unfortunate souls who went down with the ship.

His father George Barnhouse claimed £70 from the White Star Line and testified that he had been financially dependent on his deceased son, who had regularly sent him sums of money in either stamps or postal orders to pay his rent of three shillings a week (15p). A letter he had received was produced in evidence. Dated December 1908, it had been sent while his son was receiving hospital treatment for an accident and signed 'From your loving son, Robert Barnhouse'. However, Edith Curtis appeared for the defendants and claimed that the letter was in her handwriting – as 'Charles' could neither read or write. She contested that she had dealt with all of the late seaman's correspondence and had never sent any money on his behalf to the natural parents. Furthermore, Charles Barnes had only worked for eighteen months out of the last four years of his life. During these long periods of unemployment she had supported him, yet, despite always treating him 'like one of my own children', her own claim for compensation had been rejected by the White Star Line.

Summing up the case, Judge Lush-Wilson paid tribute to Mrs Curtis for her 'extraordinary kindness' to the deceased. In that respect, he considered that the dead man's obligations had been almost greater to her than his own parents. Although, the uncorroborated claims of George Barnhouse were 'vague and shadowy', nevertheless, he found the applicant 'an honest and

Barnes 'gave up the drink' and went to sea on the doomed ship.

truthful witness' and although, the sum of £70 requested was 'altogether too high' awarded the sum of £5 plus costs.

Edith Curtis hinted that Charles Barnes had been involved in petty crime, stating that he was 'always in trouble' but since he 'gave up the drink' had become 'a different man'. Sadly, this change in his personal situation had seemingly enabled him to resume his career at sea and gain a position on the doomed *Titanic*.

LORRAINE ALLISON
BACK FROM THE DEAD

'Lorraine Allison, long believed to have been drowned in the Titanic*... still is alive'*

In the aftermath of the maritime tragedy, some curious murder cases emerged involving three passengers on the *Titanic*. One of these was Oskar Palmquist, a twenty-six-year-old Swedish immigrant travelling to join his siblings in Connecticut, who had a remarkable escape when he was rescued after spending hours in the

Oskar Palmquist survived for six hours in the water.

icy waters. It was therefore surprising when his body was discovered in only six feet of water at Bunnell's Pond on the Pequonnock River in April 1925. He had been missing for a month and was presumed to have accidentally drowned, but in 1998, his descendants revealed a long-held belief that had come down through the family alleging that his death had been no accident, but murder. According to this unsubstantiated theory, Oskar's head was held deliberately beneath the water by a jealous love rival, with whom he had been vying for the affections of a woman in his life. Appropriately, one definition of the word 'Pequonnock' is 'a place of slaughter'.

Unrequited love was at the centre of another mysterious death, when Gertrude Klaber, the widow of *Titanic* victim, Herbert Klaber, was reported to have been shot and killed two weeks after

Nurse Alice Cleaver and baby Trevor Allison.

remarrying in February 1914. The shocking murder was allegedly committed by a former suitor and took place at the couple's honeymoon hotel in San Francisco. However, the press had been misinformed, for, the victim of this tragedy was in fact, the unfortunate niece of Gertrude Klaber.

Another case of mistaken identity occurred when children's nurse, Alice Cleaver, escaped from the sinking ship with the youngest child in her care, eleven-month-old Trevor Allison. Seemingly, in the panic to reach the lifeboats, the nurse became separated from her employers, Hudson and Bess Allison, who subsequently perished along with their three-year-old daughter, Lorraine – the only child travelling first class to lose her life. Over the years, the name of nanny Alice Catherine Cleaver, became linked by intrepid *Titanic* researchers with convicted murderer Alice Mary Cleaver, an unmarried domestic servant who was sentenced to death for throwing her unwanted infant son out of a train window while travelling on the North London Railway in 1909. The killer was reprieved and given a life sentence, then died as a prison inmate. The two Alice Cleavers were both aged twenty-two in 1912, so it is little wonder that the belief persists that a child murderer had been taken on as a children's nurse. However, the good name of Alice Catherine Cleaver was besmirched further by false accusations that, when the ship was foundering, she abandoned Trevor Allison to his fate, forcing his frantic parents to search in vain for their infant son until it was too late to save themselves. The case took another twist when a woman claiming to be Lorraine Allison suddenly 'surfaced' to claim an inheritance in 1940. Trevor Allison, whom Alice Cleaver had rescued from the *Titanic*, had died of ptomaine poisoning in 1929, leaving his guardians, Hudson Allison's brother George and his wife Lillian, as chief beneficiaries of the Allison estate in Montreal. George Allison subsequently died and, according to the press, his widow 'was stirred today by the prospect that Lorraine Allison, long believed to have been drowned in the *Titanic* disaster of 1912, still is alive'. Mrs Lorraine Kramer claimed that as little Lorraine Allison, she had been handed to a male passenger named Hyde who had taken her to safety and then raised her in the American Midwest. The far-fetched story purported that the Mr Hyde who had saved her was in fact, Thomas Andrews, the designer of the *Titanic*, who had also been thought lost in the disaster. According to Lorraine Kramer's wild tale, she had shared a cabin on the rescue ship *Carpathia* with Thomas Andrews and Bruce Ismay, the disgraced chairman of the White Star Line, who paid Andrews to disappear so that he could not testify that the *Titanic* was travelling too fast through the ice field. Now known as Mr Hyde, Andrews spent the rest of his life moving from town to town with the little girl whom he adopted. The pair were periodically visited by Bruce Ismay and George Allison who both carried on paying 'hush' money. The former to try and salvage his tattered reputation, the latter to keep the child away from the Allison inheritance.

Although, Lorraine Kramer eventually dropped her long legal battle to be recognised as a member of the Allison family in 1951, there remains a remarkable coincidence with the case of killer Alice Mary Cleaver. When arrested, the child murderer denied the charges brought against her, maintaining that she had given up her two-month-old baby to a 'Mrs Gray' at an orphanage in London. Similarly, Lorraine Kramer claimed that she had often met the sister of Thomas Andrews. Incredibly, this mysterious lady was also known as 'Mrs Gray', stimulating misguided suspicions that the false claimant had been coached by the woman with inside knowledge of the Allison family – their former nanny, Alice Catherine Cleaver.

KATHERINE SCOTT
DOUBLE TRAGEDY

*'You are loved and respected in England in a way
that makes me very happy'*

Polar explorer and national hero Sir Ernest Shackleton was called as an expert witness at the British Inquiry. Having sailed through ice floes on many occasions during his expeditions, his evidence was sought on the danger of icebergs. In his opinion: 'I think the possibility of accident is greatly enhanced by the speed at which the ship goes. I was in a ship specially built for ice but I took the precaution to slow down'. In such conditions, Shackleton cautiously reduced the vessel's speed to two knots, whilst the *Titanic* had been steaming ahead at twenty knots. Lord Mersey, presiding over the inquiry, agreed that 'excessive speed' had contributed largely to the sinking, but was inclined to think that Captain Smith had simply made an 'error of judgement' as he was reluctant to find a man guilty of 'negligence' when he was not alive to answer the charge.

With Captain Smith's reputation intact, eminent sculptor Katherine Scott was commissioned to produce a life-size statue of Captain Smith later erected in Beacon Park, Lichfield, the seat of the diocese where Smith was born. Immortalised in bronze, the plaque beneath the figure reads that he bequeathed to his countrymen 'the memory and example of a great heart, a brave life and a heroic death' – sentiments that also apply to the sculptor's famous husband, explorer Robert Falcon Scott, who, unbeknown to her and

Captain Smith: 'a great heart, a brave life and a heroic death'.

the world at large, had died two weeks before the maritime tragedy. Faced with severe storms and blizzards whist returning from his ill-fated expedition to the South Pole, Scott perished only eleven miles from safety. The leader's diary revealed that he was the last one of the five-man party to die on 29 March, although, the truth was not discovered until a search party recovered the bodies in November 1912. Widowed Kathleen Scott subsequently undertook the task of creating artistic memorials to her husband that were unveiled in London, Portsmouth and Christchurch, New Zealand.

Antarctic explorer Captain Robert Falcon Scott completed his journey to the South Pole in January 1912. After successfully reaching his destination, he was disappointed to discover that Roald Amundsen and his party had become the first men to reach the pole only one month earlier. The Norwegian explorer Amundsen had secretly switched his attention to the South Pole when American Robert Peary became the first man to reach the North Pole in 1909. On 8 October 1912, unaware of Scott's tragic fate, his unwitting wife wrote a final letter to him the day after showing a fund-raising film, ironically made in Norway, of the team training for the expedition, to a select audience in London. After commenting about the success

An advert for sponsors of Scott's training exercise in Norway – the homeland of Amundsen who won the race to the South Pole.

of the event and expecting that it would be 'quite a few months' before he received her letter she wrote:

> Lambie dear, there's another thing I want to impress upon you – I don't know whether you have just heard the Amundsen news or whether you learnt it at the Pole (neither bear thinking of) but I want to tell you with six months knowledge of it upon one that it matters very very little – so far less than one thought at first – indeed in some respects it has done good for it has laid great stress on the differences of the two ventures & the greater scientific importance of yours is percolating into the public mind in a manner it never would have done had not contrast been shown – upon my word I don't think it has made a scrap of difference. I couldn't have believed it would matter so little.

Of course everybody says he [Amundsen] didn't play the game, but I can make myself see another point of view – If a man is doing anything that only one man can do – be the first man to invent anything, first man to find gold, first man to perform some long thought of operation etc., etc., galore. Anything wherein the main shout is in being first he does not perhaps apprise all the people working along the same lines as his progress and intents, and yet no one thinks his gains ill gotten – It is only a point of view.

Oh my darling how I love you and long to talk with you and know that you are content. You're not going to let the little Amundsen pinprick (upon my word it's no more) worry you, are you? It looked huge when it first met the eye and has now dwindled into nothing.

You are loved and respected in England in a way that makes me very happy. To see your little face in the Cinematograph last night, almost like a stranger after all these years, and your dear toes when you took off your socks then to feel that in a few short months – !

Don't ever be sad, my darling, life is ever so glorious. I'm so happy everybody is so nice to me for your sake I like to know and our little home's so nice and my work prospers and I'm so well and Peter [their only child who would become a famous naturalist] so magnificent & you're coming home to us.

Dejected to discover that they had lost the race to the South Pole, Scott and his four companions perished from hunger and exposure before they could reach the safety of a food and fuel depot. In a tragedy that eerily foreshadowed the fate of the *Titanic*, the leader of the Antarctic expedition wrote a final message in his diary, which, also serves as a fitting tribute to Captain Smith and the poor souls who drowned in the icy waters of the Atlantic: 'Had we lived I should have had a tale to tell of the hardiest endurance and courage of my companions which would have stirred the heart of every Englishman'.

JACK JOHNSON
FARE THEE WELL, *TITANIC*

'We are not hauling no coal'

Legendary blues singer Huddie Leadbetter, known professionally as 'Leadbelly', wrote a song called *Titanic* relating that there was one man with good reason to be relieved he had not sailed on the vessel's maiden voyage as he had planned. The lyric alleges that black world heavyweight boxing champion Jack Johnson had been refused passage on the doomed vessel because of the colour of his skin:

> Jack Johnson want to get on board,
> Captain said, 'I ain't hauling no coal',
> Cryin', 'Fare thee, *Titanic*, fare thee well',
> Jack Johnson heard the mighty shock
> Mighta seen him doin' the Eagle Rock
> Cryin', 'Fare thee, *Titanic*, fare thee well'.

In a letter to the head of his record company, Moses Asch, Leadbelly explained the story behind the song:

> When they was getting on board [there] was not no coloured folks on. There was not no Negroes that died on that ship. But Jack Johnson went to get on board. 'We are not hauling no coal', [said Captain Smith]. So Jack Johnson didn't like what the Big Boss said. He went and tried to do something

Jack Johnson behind bars in 1920.

about it, but it was so much Jim Crow he could have no go. And a few hours later Jack Johnson read the papers where the *Titanic* went down. Then the peoples began to holler about that mighty shock. You might have seen Jack Johnson doing the Eagle Rock [a popular dance of the time] so glad that he was not on that ship.

American Jack Johnson fought prejudice as well as boxers to become the first black heavyweight champion of the world. Fears of the challenge to white supremacy in his homeland meant that he was denied the opportunity of fighting for the title for a decade until Canadian Tommy Burns became champion. Finally winning his chance, Johnson knocked out Burns in Australia on Boxing Day 1908. Hated by white Americans for his success, arrogance and wealth, Johnson also had a succession of inter-racial marriages which outraged people, black and white, that eventually led to his arrest on trumped-up immorality charges.

Shortly after his second wife, Etta, had committed suicide by shooting herself in the head in September 1912, Johnson began a relationship with eighteen-year-old white prostitute Lucille Cameron who became his 'business secretary'. When her mother heard the news she informed the police that her daughter had been abducted. Johnson was tried and discharged, but was then deemed to have previously broken the law for taking a scorned lover, Belle Schreiber, across a state line for 'immoral purposes'. The governor of South Carolina summed up the welter of racial hatred when he said, 'If we cannot protect our white women from black fiends like Johnson, where is our boasted civilisation.' Meanwhile, Johnson had wed Cameron and, while out on bail, he fled the country with his bride. For the next seven years the champion lived in exile until he gave himself up and served his sentence of one year and a day in 1920.

Huddie Ledbetter also had his share of fights. He earned the nickname 'Leadbelly' after being shot in the stomach. His violent temper often got him into trouble with the law. In 1917, having already escaped from a chain gang where he was serving time for assaulting a woman, he shot and killed one of his friends who pulled a gun in an argument over another girl. Charged with murder and sentenced to thirty years imprisonment, the killer was fortunate to be paroled eight years later in 1925. However, he was back inside five years later for attempted murder in a knife fight, where his talent was recognised as the 'singing convict' leading to an international reputation as the 'King of the Twelve-String Guitar'.

Leadbelly's song *Titanic* perpetuated one of the great myths about the maritime disaster, for it is known one black passenger, Joseph Laroche from Haiti, died on the vessel. And there is no evidence that Jack Johnson attempted to travel on the *Titanic*. However, he continued to suffer racial prejudice all his life and it inadvertently

Leadbelly: the 'singing convict'.

brought about his death in 1946. The former champion had a fatal car crash when he angrily sped away from a restaurant that refused to serve him.

MUTINY ON THE OLYMPIC

'They were not the sort of shipmates for me'

Captain Herbert Haddock, the first master of the *Titanic* following her launch in Belfast, took over as skipper of the *Olympic*, swapping commands with Captain Edward Smith on April Fool's Day 1912. Two weeks later, whilst returning to Southampton from New York, the *Olympic* picked up distress signals from the *Titanic* 500 miles away. A rescue attempt was abandoned when the stricken vessel sank and it was felt insensitive to allow survivors in the lifeboats to see her sister ship coming over the horizon looking like the ghost of the *Titanic*.

Sister ships Olympic (left) and Titanic in Belfast.

Understandably, the disaster unnerved the crew of the *Olympic*. Following the maritime tragedy, seamen's unions demanded the provision of extra lifeboats. The White Star Line complied with the request, but, the crew were dissatisfied with the type and condition of the canvas collapsible boats supplied and, five minutes before the ship was due to sail at noon on 24 April, 300 firemen and greasers walked down the gangways and refused to sail. Non-union men with little or no seafaring experience were drafted in, causing more members of the regular crew to go on strike. Forced to abandon the voyage, officials of the White Star Line sought legal redress to punish the men for their 'mutinous behaviour'. The fifty-three men who walked out on the second occasion were arrested and brought before Portsmouth Magistrates charged with 'wilful disobedience to the lawful commands of Captain Haddock' as prescribed under the Merchant Shipping Act 1894.

Appearing for the prosecution, John Blake, superintendent engineer of the White Star Line told the court that he had recruited replacement firemen well in excess of the number required so that

the vessel could pick up the time lost in delays. This was a startling admission in light of the fact that an inquiry was in the process of exploring the loss of the *Titanic* was possibly caused by 'excessive speed'. In answer to the grievance that the 'scab labour' comprised of 'discharged convicts' and the 'dregs of Portsmouth', the official acknowledged

Was the loss of the Titanic caused by 'excessive speed'?

that the arduous nature of the work stoking furnaces in the engine room meant that it attracted men who could not find employment elsewhere. He conceded that on all the company's liners 'were men who got into jail two or three months at a time' as the shortage of applicants meant, 'I am afraid we have to take them ordinarily'. Supporting this view was second engineer Charles McKimm of the *Olympic*. Even in light of the recent disaster, he did not agree that employing 'scallywags' and 'the sort of men who spent most of their days at street corners or in the lowest class of public houses' was an undesirable policy. One of the defendants, Quartermaster George Martell, testified that Captain Haddock had told him that anyone who wanted to go ashore could do so as they could readily be replaced. Martell left the ship as he was 'thoroughly disgusted' with the appearance of the men brought aboard to replace the firemen as: 'They were not the sort of shipmates for me'.

The Bench deliberated for nearly two hours before delivering their verdict. The chairman, Sir Thomas Bramsdon, pronounced that the magistrates were satisfied that the *Olympic* was seaworthy as required by law. They also found that the men did not have the permission of the captain to go ashore, and the charge that the men had unlawfully disobeyed the lawful commands of their captain was proved. However, the court did not wish to destroy the previous good relationship that existed between captain and crew and did not think it expedient to fine or imprison the offenders whose concerns had been clearly affected by the fate of the *Titanic*. Therefore, the culprits were discharged without punishment.

The court case and the dispute resolved, Captain Haddock finally got the *Olympic* underway at midday on 15 May, when she made her sixth voyage to New York. However, the master of the ship narrowly avoided disaster seven weeks after the *Titanic* went down. Faulty navigation brought him embarrassingly close to running the ship aground on to rocks near Land's End. The incident rather proved that seamen had good reason to air their qualms about safety measures on the White Star Line.

PROPHETS OF DOOM

PULL FOR THE SHORE

Pull for the shore, sailor, pull for the shore!
Heed not the rolling waves, but bend to the oar;
Safe in the life boat, sailor, cling to self no more!
Leave the poor old stranded wreck, and pull for the shore.

Light in the darkness, sailor, day is at hand!
See o'er the foaming billows fair haven's land,
Drear was the voyage, sailor, now almost o'er,
Safe within the life boat, sailor, pull for the shore.

Trust in the life boat, sailor, all else will fail,
Stronger the surges dash and fiercer the gale,
Heed not the stormy winds, though loudly they roar;
Watch the 'bright and morning Star', and pull for the shore!

Bright gleams the morning, sailor, uplift the eye;
Clouds and darkness disappearing, glory is nigh!
Safe in the life boat, sailor, sing evermore;
'Glory, glory, hallelujah!' pull for the shore.

Phillip B. Bliss (1838-76)

CAPTAIN SMITH
THE LAST VOYAGE

'In all my experiences I have never been in an accident of any sort'

With the benefit of hindsight, many commentators viewed it as an ill-omen that Captain Edward Smith was appointed master of the *Titanic*. Boasting a previously unblemished career record of over forty years at sea, he had suddenly experienced a run of misfortune commanding the new generation of ocean-going giants produced for the White Star Line.

Appointed commodore of the White Star Line in 1904, Smith routinely took charge of the newest ships on their maiden voyages. Bad luck came thick and fast, starting with an incident in September 1911 when his vessel, the *Olympic*, crashed into the British cruiser HMS *Hawke* in the Solent. The following February, the *Olympic* struck what was believed to be a submerged wreck, and lost a blade from one of her propellers, making it necessary for repairs to be carried out in dry dock. On 10 April, as the *Titanic* set sail on her ill-fated maiden voyage, there was an embarrassing incident when she narrowly missed colliding with the American liner *New York*, which was pulled from her anchorage by suction from the gigantic vessel.

The day before, Chief Officer Henry Wilde had been transferred from the *Olympic* to the *Titanic*. Two years earlier he had lost his wife and newborn twins and soon his remaining four children would be fatherless. Wilde immediately had serious qualms about his new berth. When the ship reached Queenstown (now Cobh, County Cork) he posted a letter outlining his misgivings to his sister, 'I still don't like this ship... I have a queer feeling about it'.

In 1907, while commanding the *Adriatic* on its maiden trip, Smith commented on his excellent career as a seafarer: 'When anyone asks me how I can best describe my experiences of nearly forty years at sea I merely say "Uneventful". Of course there have been winter gales and storms and fogs and the like, but in all my experiences I have never been in an accident of any sort worth speaking about. I have seen but one vessel in distress in all my years at sea, a brig, the crew of which was taken off in a small boat in charge of my third officer. I never saw a wreck and have never been wrecked, nor was I ever in any predicament that threatened to end in a disaster of any sort. You see, I am not very good material for a story.' Smith's memory conveniently glossed over the fact that he had in fact been involved in a few notable incidents. In 1889, while in charge of the *Republic*, she ran aground for five hours off Sandy Hook on the approach to New York and, after landing her passengers, three men were killed and seven injured when a fractured furnace flue exploded. A year later, commanding the *Coptic*, as they were leaving Rio Janeiro for Plymouth, Smith ran the ship aground on Main Island. Then, while captain of the *Majestic* in 1901, a fire broke out that took five hours to extinguish as the ship approached New York.

Captain Edward Smith declared that his career had been 'uneventful'.

Aged sixty-two, Captain Smith planned to retire upon his return to England on the *Titanic*, allowing him more time to spend with his family. When the *Titanic* sailed, Edward and Eleanor Smith had a fourteen-year-old daughter, Helen Melville Smith, who was destined to suffer a series of tragic losses in her life. Following the death of her father at sea, 'Mel's' mother was subsequently knocked down and killed by a taxi in 1931. Helen reputedly married the youngest skipper in the merchant navy, Captain John Gilbertson, who died at sea having contracted blackwater fever during a voyage home from India on board his ship the *Morozan*. Another marriage to Sidney Russell-Cooke ended tragically when he was killed in an hunting accident. The couple had twins; Simon, who was killed in action during the Second World War and Priscilla who contracted the disease polio and succumbed in 1947.

Dubbed the 'grand old man of the sea' Edward Smith had unshakeable faith in the belief that modern vessels were unsinkable: 'Shipbuilding is such a perfect art nowadays that absolute disaster, involving the passengers, is inconceivable. Whatever happens, there will be time enough before the vessel sinks to save the life of everyone on board. I will go a bit further. I cannot imagine any condition that would cause the vessel to founder. Modern shipbuilding has gone beyond that'. He had clearly forgotten a golden rule of the White Star Line posted on the bridge of every vessel: 'Overconfidence – a most fruitful source of accidents, should be especially guarded against'.

Following the tragedy, caused when the skipper refused to reduce speed despite warnings about the presence of ice, newspapers on both sides of the Atlantic revealed that at a gathering of the *Olympic* officers and their wives, Captain Smith was congratulated upon the announcement that he was soon to take command of the *Titanic*. The conversation then turned to a recently published prediction mirroring the fictional short story *Futility* written in 1898 by Morgan Robertson, a popular American writer of sea adventures, in which, uncannily, a ship named *Titan*, the largest passenger ship ever built, sails in April carrying too few lifeboats as the vessel is considered unsinkable. She then strikes an iceberg on her starboard side at midnight and sinks with huge loss of life. Captain Smith responded prophetically to the suggestion, 'Well, if the largest liner in the world sinks, I shall go with it'.

JOHN JACOB ASTOR
THE JUDGEMENT OF GOD

'This calamity ought to be a lesson to men like Astor'

The wealthiest man on the *Titanic* was Colonel John Jacob Astor, whose body was found floating in the water with $2,500 on his person. Worth in excess of $100,000,000, the multi-millionaire was a veteran of the 1898 Spanish-American War in Cuba, serving his country voluntarily as he expressed a wish to live a useful life and his belief in the saying that without substance: 'Wealth is Nothing'.

Astor had experienced previous perils at sea. In 1905, his yacht *Nourmahal* foundered on a reef off Rhode Island. For nine hours, the

Astor salutes farewell to his Maker.

The Astors kiss goodbye.

steamer was pounded against the rocks before Astor managed to break free. He was also the hero of an ocean scare in 1910. Missing for two days he was feared lost, but survived having successfully steered his yacht *Noma* through a hurricane in the Caribbean. His luck ran out on the *Titanic* as he faced death bravely, standing on the deck and giving a final salute before meeting his Maker as the stricken ship made her final plunge beneath the waves.

In 1909, scandal had ruined Astor's reputation when he was divorced by his wife of twenty years over his relationship with teenager Madeline Force, whom he married two years later. Aged eighteen, the bride was nearly thirty years her husband's junior and had first caught the eye of Astor's son from his first marriage, Vincent Astor, who was slightly younger than his new stepmother. The newlyweds left America to avoid the gossip surrounding their relationship and after an extended honeymoon were returning to New York on the *Titanic*. The pregnant bride was rescued and subsequently gave birth to a son, John Jacob Astor junior, in August 1912. Although Madeline had received a $2,000,00 wedding settlement, under the terms of her late husband's will, the young widow was required to relinquish the family mansion and the income from a £5,000,000 trust fund if she ever remarried. She wasted no time in giving up financial security for love when she married banker, William Dick, during the First World War. They had known each other from childhood but the marriage ended in divorce in 1933. Happiness continued to elude Madeline when a third union to boxer and actor Enzo Fiermonte ended in 1938. Two years later, heart problems of a medical kind brought about the end of her life at the age of only forty-seven – the same age that her first husband had reached when he met his death on the *Titanic*.

John Jacob Astor's second marriage had been denounced by the clergy of his Episcopal faith which forbade the remarriage of a divorced person at fault. One of the fiercest critics was Dr Richmond, rector of a church in Philadelphia. He preached a red-hot sermon when the couple announced their betrothal. Later, he publicly declared his belief that it was the hand of providence that had sent Colonel Astor to a watery grave:

> The death of Col. John Jacob Astor at sea in the going down of the *Titanic* preaches a great gospel of God's power to us all. There are forces in life which demand recognition and obedience. Mr Astor and his crowd of New York and Newport associates have for years paid not the slightest attention to the laws of church or state which have seemed to contravene their personal pleasures or sensual delights.
>
> But you can't defy God all the time. The day of reckoning comes and comes not in our own way. In another world Astor will do penance. Without his millions and bereft of his great estate, which yielded him his means for a continual carousel, he will begin a new life.
>
> There are a lot more like Astor in New York and in Newport, but the number is decreasing. The only remedy is to set the moral standards so high that these men will not dare to defy the laws of the country, as these sensualists have done.
>
> This calamity ought to be a lesson to men like Astor. Our sympathy for the dead causes us to stifle moral judgement for the men of high positions and the courses they should pursue.

WALLACE HARTLEY
NEARER MY GOD TO THEE

Nearer, My God, to Thee, nearer to Thee!
E'en though it be a cross that raiseth me
Still all my song shall be
Nearer my God, to thee,
Nearer, My God, to thee, nearer to thee!

One of the tributes paid to the remarkable self-sacrifice of music director Wallace Hartley and his band of musicians who calmly carried on playing while the lifeboats were being lowered, appeared in the *Denver Post*:

THERE IS SOMETHING IN MUSIC THAT MAKES MEN BRAVE

> In 1776 the men with the fife and drum led the charge up to the cannon's mouth playing 'Yankee Doodle'.
> In 1898 the band belonging to the First Colorado volunteers led the charge that resulted in the fall of Manila, and during the rain of bullets played 'Hot Time'.
> In 1912 while the *Titanic* was making her last struggle against the sea that was sure to conquer, the band of the vessel stood on the deck playing 'Nearer, My God, To Thee'.

A legend was born when several passengers recalled hearing the poignant hymn, although army officer, Colonel Archie Gracie, reputedly the last survivor to leave the ship after leaping into the water at the last moment from the deck where the band had been playing, wryly observed: 'If "Nearer, My God, To Thee" was one of the selections, I would surely have noticed it and regarded it as a tactless warning of immediate death, and more likely to create a panic.'

As passengers streamed from their staterooms to the lifeboats the band struck up light, cheerful music – ragtime, waltzes, music hall ditties, from their repertoire of 350 popular songs, but the abiding memory is of the musicians carrying on playing with the water virtually up to their knees before perishing beneath the waves playing sacred music. As the strains of *Nearer, My God, To Thee* died away, people in the lifeboats began to sing the gospel hymn *Pull For the Shore* in order to keep up their spirits and drown out the harrowing screams of the dying. Wallace Hartley's corpse was recovered from the ocean. Strapped to his body was his precious violin. The case was stamped with his initials and an inscription from his fiancée: 'For Wallace on the occasion of our engagement from Maria.' A statue was erected to honour Hartley's memory in his birthplace where 30,000 mourners lined the route at his civic funeral in the small cotton town of Colne, Lancashire. A few days later, a memorial concert to the

Heroic Bandmaster Wallace Hartley.

Titanic bandsmen, held at the Albert Hall in London, featured seven of world's leading orchestras. The event culminated in a deeply emotional moment when the audience of 10,000 people sang in unison the tune that had become the world's most famous hymn. As *Nearer, My God, To Thee* rang out, people wept and attention was drawn to two ladies who were special guests. A *Daily Sketch* reporter revealed: 'The last time they had heard it was from a small boat laden to the water's edge and the band was playing the hymn on the boat-deck of the sinking Titanic'.

The same newspaper had earlier revealed that Wallace Hartley had once discussed this outcome with fellow musician, Mr E. Moody of Leeds, who told a reporter that the conductor had a presentiment that one day he would meet his end at sea while the two men were playing in a band together on the Cunard liner *Mauretania*:

> 'I do not know what made me say it', said Mr Moody, 'but one night when Hartley and I were walking round the *Mauretania*'s deck together I suddenly asked, 'What would you do, old chap, if you were on board a liner that was rapidly sinking?'
>
> 'I'd get my men together and play' he replied without hesitation.
>
> 'What would you play?' I asked.
>
> 'Well' he said 'I don't think I could do better than play "Oh God Our Help in Ages Past" or "Nearer, My God, To Thee". They are both favourite hymns of mine, and they would be very suitable to the occasion'.

WILLIAM STEAD

A MESSAGE FROM BEYOND
THE GRAVE

'Let us consider the Atlantic as the grave.'

The world's most famous journalist, William Stead, pioneered the use of sensational bold headlines, pictorial illustrations and provocative leading articles as editor of London's influential *Pall Mall Gazette*. The newspaper was an organ of the Liberal Party led by William Gladstone, who was to later regret recommending Stead for the post, as the new editor was a leading exponent of the 'new journalism' or 'shock journalism', agitating for social reforms and endeavouring to make the newspaper 'the tribune of the poor'.

The crusading editor took a proactive approach and his finest piece of investigative journalism appeared in July 1885 when he exposed the horrors of child prostitution in London. In a series of articles entitled *The Maiden Tribute of Modern Babylon* he described how he had bought a thirteen year-old girl from her mother to demonstrate how easily the depraved lust for a virgin could be satisfied in the sex trade. The campaign forced the government to swiftly introduce legislation raising the age of consent to sixteen years, but, not before Stead was arrested on ludicrous charges of abducting a minor without her father's consent, for which, he was sentenced to three months imprisonment. On each anniversary of this blatant miscarriage of justice, Stead would proudly appear in public wearing a prison uniform.

William Stead requested 'Nearer, My God, To Thee'.

William Stead was a fervent believer in psychic phenomena and predicted that his own death would come about by drowning. It came to pass that he lost his life while travelling on the *Titanic* to address a conference organised by the 'Man and Religious Forward Movement' in New York. The impending maritime disaster and his tragic fate had been addressed in his writings. In his book on spiritualism *How I Know the Dead Return*, one paragraph begins 'Let us consider the Atlantic as the grave.' The author then compares one shore with Earth and the other with the Eternal shore. In March 1886, he published a fictitious article entitled *How the Mail Steamer Went Down in Mid-Atlantic, by a Survivor*. In the story an unnamed steamer collides with another ship and due to a shortage of lifeboats there is a huge loss of life. Stead comments 'this is exactly what might take place and will take place if liners are sent to sea short of boats.' Uncannily, the event that sent him to a watery grave was graphically prophesised twenty years before his death in an article published in the December 1892 issue of the *Review of Reviews* – an international monthly magazine founded by him. In a tale entitled *From the Old World to the New*, Stead describes how a White Star liner, the *Majestic*, is carrying a group of English tourists across the Atlantic to visit the World Fair in Chicago when, one of the passengers, a clairvoyant, picks up a telepathic message from a friend who is close to death and floating helplessly in the water having survived the wreck of the *Montrose*, sunk after colliding with a giant iceberg that can be seen from the *Majestic*. The clairvoyant persuades the captain to put him out on a boat and his powers guide him to rescue the survivor. The setting of the story and the descriptions of the iceberg and the wrecked ship tally almost exactly with the fate of the *Titanic* – although by 1912, Marconi's wireless telegraphy, not telepathy, sent an SOS to summon rescue.

In the midst of the biggest news story of the century, the journalist calmly helped women and children into the lifeboats, secure in his belief that there was nothing to fear from his impending death. Psychic societies on both sides of the Atlantic reportedly anticipated contact from beyond the grave and a month after William Stead's passing, a Scottish medium, Mrs Coates, claimed to have conducted a psychic interview with the spirit of her personal friend who relayed to her a message revealing that it was he who had made a last request to the band of the *Titanic* to play the scared hymn *Nearer, My God, To Thee*.

DR WILLIAM MINAHAN
THE GYPSY'S CURSE

'Be Brave.'

In the aftermath of the *Titanic* disaster, strange stories emerged from people who had apparently been forewarned that the great ship was predestined to sink on its maiden voyage. One of those who lived to tell the tale was the Hon. J. C. Middleton of Cleveland, vice-president of the Akron-Canton Railway of Ohio, who revealed to his wife and friends, several days before due to sail, that he had cancelled the passage after experiencing a terrifying dream on two consecutive nights: 'I booked a cabin in the *Titanic* on March 23. I felt unaccountably depressed at the time, and on 3 April I dreamt that I saw the *Titanic* capsized in mid-ocean and hundreds of people struggling frantically in the water. The next day I dreamt exactly the same dream.' A number of well-known people vouched for Mr Middleton's reason for his change of plan and one of them voluntarily signed a sworn affidavit to that effect.

Another passenger who did not believe in portents and omens was not so fortunate. He perished when he ignored a gypsy's warning. One of the most prominent surgeons in Wisconsin, Dr William Minahan, died aged forty-four returning on the *Titanic* from a trip to Europe accompanied by his wife Lillian and sister Daisy who both survived the tragedy.

Dr Minahan's death fulfilled a prediction that he would die in a maritime disaster made by a soothsayer five years earlier, when he and a group of friends visited a gypsy camp to have their fortunes

The capsized Titanic *was seen in a dream.*

told. When the doctor's palm was read, he was informed he would meet his end on a steamer during his second trip abroad. Shortly afterwards, the physician journeyed to Europe and spent a year conducting medical research. When he planned his second trip in January 1912, his friends jokingly reminded him of the gypsy's prediction of death. Although Dr Minahan ridiculed the suggestion of his impending doom, he took the precaution of arranging his affairs before sailing and took out personal life insurance of $100,000 and accident insurance of $60,000. The Minahans booked a voyage abroad to visit members of their family living in Ireland, before boarding the *Titanic* for the fateful return journey at Queenstown.

Dr Minahan's body was recovered and buried in Wisconsin, but the gypsy's curse seemingly continued to affect other members of his family with tragic results. In 1915, William Minahan's brother, physician Dr John Minahan, lost his wife when she was struck by a train near their home. An investigation failed to establish whether her death was due to accident or design. There was no question that it was suicide when their son John junior ended his life at the age of twenty-one by firing a bullet into his brain while studying at the University of Chicago in 1923. He had discussed suicide with fellow students at his fraternity house after being jilted by a girlfriend. Two years later, Dr John Minahan, hurried to Juneau Park, Milwaukee, driven by a premonition that 'something dreadful had happened' after reading a newspaper report that an unidentified young man had shot and killed himself there. The victim proved to be his youngest son, Robert, a twenty-one-year-old medical student at Northwestern University. In this fourth avoidable tragedy to strike the Minahan family, it was revealed that the untimely death of the university freshman had not been brought about by unrequited love or grief for the loss of his mother and brother, but an argument over money matters with his devastated father. Perhaps Dr John Minahan was fortified by his brother William's last words to the ladies as they stepped into a lifeboat on the *Titanic*, 'Be Brave'.

MARGARET BROWN
HEROINE OF THE TITANIC

'She had evil forebodings that something might happen.'

A wild rumour circulated, attempting to explain the death of an 'unsinkable' ship, that the infamous Hope Diamond had been secretly transported back to America on the *Titanic* by a passenger returning from Amsterdam, where the large blue diamond had been reset for its owner, Evalyn McLean, of Washington. Said to be the unluckiest stone in the world, dire consequences had reputedly befallen its owners since it had been allegedly plucked and stolen from the forehead of an idol in India by Jean Baptiste Tavernier who sold it to his ill-fated monarch Louis LXIV in 1668. Subsequently, from the days when it shone on the neck of Queen Marie Antoinette, then later sold to pay off the debts created by the wanton lifestyle of King George IV following his death in 1830, the legend persisted that ill-fortune would visit anyone who came into contact with the gem. The press speculated that had it really been transported on the *Titanic*, its presence, if known, would have certainly unnerved superstitious passengers. However, the story proved to be without foundation as the forty-five carat jewel, surrounded by sixteen white diamonds was proved to be still in the possession of its proud and unharmed owner.

One woman who famously refused to leave the sinking ship without her jewellery was Margaret Brown who rushed back to her cabin to retrieve the precious gems. Subsequently dubbed the 'Unsinkable "Molly" Brown' in a Hollywood movie, the extraordinary luck she had enjoyed in a remarkable rags to riches life continued. She survived the tragedy when she went back up on deck and heard the cry, 'Women and children first' – later recalling how she was grabbed by a crewman and 'literally thrown into a lifeboat and lowered into the foaming sea.' In charge of the lifeboat was drunken sailor Robert Hichens who was soon put in his place: 'We stood him patiently, and then after he had told us we had no chance, told us many times, and after he had explained that we had no food, no water, and no compass I told him to be still or he would go overboard. Then he was quiet. I rowed because I would have frozen to death. I made them all row, It saved their lives.'

After rowing in freezing conditions for seven hours, the party was picked up by the rescue ship *Carpathia*. Upon reaching New York, the woman who had escaped poverty when her husband struck it rich by discovering gold in the Little Jonny mine in

Survivors on the Carpathia *reach New York.*

Leadville, Colorado, made light of her ordeal by telegraphing her lawyer in Denver: 'Water was fine and swimming good. Neptune was exceedingly kind to me and I am now high and dry.'

Before boarding the *Titanic* at Cherbourg, Margaret Brown and her daughter Helen, who was a student at the Sorbonne, had been travelling extensively throughout Europe. They were staying with honeymooners John and Madeline Astor in Egypt, when Margaret received word that her eldest grandchild, Lawrence Palmer Brown junior, was ill. Leaving Helen behind, the concerned grandmother booked her passage on the first available ship which fate decreed was the *Titanic*.

Upon reaching New York, Margaret Brown was lauded by the press for keeping spirits up in the lifeboat and encouraging the other women to row, raising $10,000 for destitute survivors from her wealthy companions on board the *Carpathia*, then rendering assistance to the point of exhaustion in hospitals caring for the recuperating occupants of the lifeboats. Helen Brown received a letter from her mother referring to her new found fame: 'I have had flowers, letters, telegrams from people until I am befuddled. They are petitioning Congress to give me a medal... If I must call a specialist to examine my head it is due to the title of Heroine of the *Titanic*.'

Margaret Brown also revealed that during her recent visit to Egypt, she had paid a fortune teller to read her palm in Cairo. The soothsayer made a grim prophecy that she was to journey on a ship that would sink resulting in many deaths. Another bad omen occurred when boarding the *Titanic* at Cherbourg, in the company of fellow passenger Emma Bucknell who declared solemnly: 'I have a premonition about this ship.' Margaret Brown recalled, 'She had evil forebodings that something might happen. We laughed at her premonitions.'

HELEN BISHOP
A THREEFOLD PROPHECY

*'We have to be rescued, for the rest of my
prophecy to come true'*

Honeymooners Dickinson and Helen Bishop were the first to leave the sinking ship. Reluctantly leaving their dog Freu Freu behind in their first class stateroom as they realised that, 'there would be little sympathy for a woman carrying a dog in her arms when there were lives of women and children to be saved,' the newlyweds climbed into a lifeboat, later claiming that they were obeying an order they heard called out that 'all brides and grooms may board.'

Helen Bishop later graphically described the terrible fate of those left behind on the doomed vessel:

> The water was like glass. There wasn't even the ripple usually found on a small lake. By the time we had pulled 100 yards the lower row of portholes had disappeared. When we were a mile away the second row had gone, but there was still no confusion. Indeed everything seemed to be quiet on the ship until her stern was raised out of the water by the list forward. Then a veritable wave of humanity surged up out of the steerage and shut the lights from our view. We were too far away to see the passengers individually, but we could see the black masses of human forms and hear their death cries and groans. For a moment the ship seemed to be pointing

Titanic *was like a whale plunging beneath the water.*

straight down, looking like a gigantic whale submerging itself, head-first.

While taking her turn on the oars, Helen Bishop kept up the spirits of her fellow survivors by relating a story about what had occurred to her during a recent trip to Egypt. There a fortune teller had predicted that she would survive a shipwreck and an earthquake before an automobile accident would end her life. Therefore, she explained, 'We have to be rescued, for the rest of my prophecy to come true.' When salvation came in the shape of a rescue ship, Helen Bishop told the press, 'My husband joined me on the *Carpathia* and we knelt together and thanked God for our preservation.' However, the couple's luck soon took a turn for the worse. Dickinson, who had inherited a fortune upon the death of his first wife, endured rumours that he had dressed as a woman in order to secure a place on the lifeboat, while Helen, who had been in the early stages of pregnancy while on the *Titanic*, suffered tragedy soon after giving birth to a baby boy, Randall Walton Bishop on 8 December 1912. Sadly, the infant survived only two days. Taking a vacation in California to try and get over their loss, the Bishops' hotel was shaken by an earthquake – fulfilling the second part of the soothsayer's prophecy.

The third part of the prophecy came to pass in November 1913. During the early hours of the morning, while returning to their home in Dowagiac, Michigan, after attending a country dance in Kalamazoo, Dickinson Bishop lost control of his speeding car and ran into a tree. The driver was virtually unharmed, but his wife was thrown twenty-five feet from the vehicle, striking her head on the pavement. Helen's injuries were pronounced fatal by doctors, but she made a miraculous recovery after having a steel plate inserted in her skull. However, the accident affected her mental faculties which brought about the end of the Bishops' marriage and the couple were divorced in January 1916. Helen had spent Christmas with friends and enjoyed many social gatherings over the festive period before taking a long winter cruise to the West Indies and Panama Canal. Upon her return she was taken ill while visiting friends in Danville, Illinois. Despite receiving treatment from two of Danville's best physicians and three specialists from Chicago, the local press reported that the twenty-three-year-old continued to 'sink' to her death. The final part of the prophecy was belatedly completed on 16 March 1916. Coincidentally, the article announcing Helen Bishop's death appeared on the front page of the local paper which, also featured news of the marriage of her former husband Dickinson Bishop to his third wife, Sidney Boyce of Chicago.

EDITH RUSSELL
DYING IN LUXURIOUS SQUALOR

'I've had every disaster but bubonic plague and a husband.'

American fashion buyer and writer Edith Rosenbaum was based in France where she was seriously injured in an automobile accident which killed her fiancée, Ludwig Loewe, a wealthy German gun manufacturer, in August 1911. Fully recovered, she planned to take a break in New York and boarded the *Titanic* at Cherbourg. However, despite the opulent surroundings, when the ship reached Ireland she wrote a letter, describing her misgivings about the voyage, to her secretary in Paris:

> This is the most wonderful boat you can think of. In length it would reach from the corner of the Rue de la Paix to about the Rue de Rivoli.
>
> Everything imaginable: swimming pool, Turkish bath, gymnasium, squash courts, cafes, tea gardens, smoking rooms, a lounge bigger than the Grand Hotel Lounge; huge drawing rooms, and bed rooms larger than in the average Paris hotel. It is a monster, and I can't say I like it, as I feel as if I were in a big hotel, instead of on a cosy ship; everyone is so stiff and formal. There are hundreds of help, bell boys, stewards, stewardesses and lifts. To say that it is wonderful, is unquestionable, but not the cosy ship-board feeling of former years. We are now off Queenstown. I just hate to leave Paris and will be jolly glad to get back again. Am going to

'I feel as if I were in a big hotel, instead of on a cosy ship.'

take my very much needed rest on this trip, but I cannot get over my feeling of depression and premonition of trouble. How I wish it were over!

Her forebodings about the vessel proved correct and when the time came to abandon ship she famously asked her steward to retrieve a treasured possession from her stateroom. A small toy pig covered with white fur named 'Maxixe' after the dance melody it played by winding its tail. The stuffed animal given to her by her mother as a 'good luck charm' did much to keep the children amused in one of the lifeboats. When she finally reached New York on the *Carpathia*, the writer defended the conduct of the chairman of the White Star Line, Bruce Ismay, who had been fiercely criticised for saving his own life at the cost of others: 'I believe that Mr Ismay must have entered his lifeboat at the very last moment, judging by the fact that I myself was among the last to leave the *Titanic*. I last saw him calling out, "Any more women? If so, all off now." I think that Mr Ismay should not be censured, as he took his chances after all the women in that part of the ship had been saved.'

Edith Rosenbaum weathered other catastrophes during an eventful and accident-prone life. 'I've been in shipwrecks, car crashes, fires, floods and tornadoes,' she was once quoted as saying,

'I've had every disaster but bubonic plague and a husband.' During the First World War, the daughter of Jewish immigrants, tactfully changed her German-sounding name from Rosenbaum to Russell and reputedly became the first female war correspondent. At the Front she bravely spent time in the trenches with the troops reporting on progress for the *New York Herald*. Moving in celebrity circles during the interwar period, she danced with Mussolini, bred dogs for Maurice Chevalier and later became godmother to the children of 'Rat Pack' actor Peter Lawford and his wife Patricia, sister of President John Kennedy. She gave many interviews about her experience on the *Titanic* and was a technical advisor on the film *A Night To Remember* released in 1958.

In complete contrast to the glamorous lifestyle she had led, Edith Russell's last years were spent as an eccentric recluse. Booking into a posh London hotel, she never left the room and refused to let anyone enter to clean. Anyone who upset the cantankerous guest were threatened with lawsuits. Dying in April 1975 at the age of ninety-sixty in luxurious squalor, Edith was not missed by the hotel staff who had suffered from her bizarre behaviour. Upon hearing about the celebrity's death, a maid commented to a London reporter that 'Old Edy was the contrariest old hag whatever crossed my path.'

THE ADMIRABLE CRICHTON

'He would be on deck doing his duty until the end.'

Major Archibald Butt's eulogy was delivered by President William Taft when the White House received confirmation of the loss of his aide-de camp in the Atlantic: 'I never really had any hope of seeing him again. Archie was a soldier, and he was always where he was wanted. When I heard that the *Titanic* had sunk with fifteen hundred souls, I knew that Major Butt would be among them. He would be on deck doing his duty until the end.'

Presidential aide Archibald Butt.

An influential military aide, firstly to President Theodore Roosevelt, then his successor, President William Taft, Archibald Butt was born into a prominent family. After graduating from university in 1888, he began a career in journalism, later based in Washington as correspondent sending dispatches to a group of newspapers south of the Mason-Dixon line. In 1898 Butt entered the United States army as a lieutenant during the Spanish-American War, and then served in campaigns in the Philippines and Cuba before being appointed military aide to 'Teddy' Roosevelt in 1908. Developing his personal role much further in Taft's administration, the major accompanied the President on all his travels becoming his friend

Major Butt depicted holding back passengers at gunpoint.

and confidante, combining all the best qualities of aide-de-camp, military advisor, diplomat and secretary. Due to the pressure of work and his attempts to diffuse a bitter personal quarrel between Roosevelt and Taft, Major Butt's health began to deteriorate early in 1912. Persuaded that he needed rest, he took six weeks leave from the White House and sailed for Europe with his close friend, the artist, Francis Millet, who was en-route to Rome on business before he too perished on the *Titanic*. While in Rome, Butt combined pleasure with business. Granted an audience with the Pope, he presented the pontiff with a confidential letter from President Taft expressing his gratitude for the recent creation of three new American cardinals.

On the fateful night that the *Titanic* sank, Major Butt dined at the captain's table, then emerged as one of the heroes of the ensuing tragedy. With calm authority, he deterred crazed men from attempting to join the women and children in the lifeboats. Press reports claimed that his last goodbye was paid to Miss Marie Young, whom he had met at the White House where she had formerly been a music teacher to the Roosevelt children. She found a place in a lifeboat and recalled: 'Major Butt escorted me to a seat in the bow. He helped me find a space, arranged my clothing about me, stood erect, doffed his hat and smiled and said "Good-bye". And then he stepped back to the deck, already awash. As we rowed away we looked back, and the last I saw of him he was smiling and waving his hand to me.' Another survivor, Dr Washington Dodge, saw the figures of Major Butt and Colonel Astor silhouetted against the sky, heads erect, their arms apparently around each others shoulders, standing on the bridge as the stricken vessel plunged beneath the waves.

The chivalrous officer's genial nature and devotion to duty in presidential circles led Major Butt to be regarded as an 'Admirable Crichton', but, unlike the fictional character in the stage play created by J. M. Barrie, when Archie was involved in a shipwreck, he did not survive. Furthermore, the press revealed that, prior to leaving Washington for the last time, the gallant major had received a mysterious warning that he would die during his trip to Europe. Prior to sailing abroad, he experienced a premonition that he might not return alive and contacted his lawyer to draw up a will and wind up his affairs in preparation for his impending predicted death.

HENRY FORBES JULIAN
UNLUCKY THIRTEEN

'Quit you like men, be strong.'

Distinguished mining consultant, Henry Forbes Julian, who had worked on three continents and invented an electrical method of extracting and separating gold and silver, was due to travel to San Francisco on a business trip and booked a passage on the *Olympic* leaving Southampton on 3 April 1912. Fate intervened to disrupt his plans when a booklet on metallurgy he had written for his employer was delayed at the printer's causing him to reschedule his passage. His wife was too ill to travel with him as she had contracted influenza, but once aboard the *Titanic*, Julian met up with an old mining friend, Colonel John Weir, who had transferred from the liner *Philadephia* whose sailing had been postponed due to a national coal strike .

The year 1912 was the tenth anniversary of Forbes Julian's marriage to Hester Pengelly, daughter of eminent geologist William Pengelly. The lady had also written a memoir to her late father to commemorate the jubilee of the Devonshire Association,

Hester Forbes Julian experienced a terrible premonition.

founded by him in July 1862 to conduct research. Hester's husband's plans to return from his transatlantic trip in time for the jubilee celebration were thwarted by events that were foreseen by her when she experienced a terrible premonition at their home in Torquay:

> Descended from a long line of sailors and living by the sea and loving it, the present writer had always gladly accompanied her husband on his voyages; nor had she previously felt any anxiety about him when on the ocean. But on the night of Sunday, April 14th, after retiring to rest she was filled with some presentiment of coming evil and felt too anxious to be able to sleep. Rising up again before midnight, she continued for a long time reading prayers, especially those appointed to be used at sea. Eagerly inquiring the next morning from the servants if any news had come and scanning the papers, she was temporarily reassured, for the intelligence of the catastrophe did not reach her until the afternoon. But surely a guiding influence must have directed her thoughts, and some projection of the mind into space must have enabled her in some mysterious way to hold communion with one far distant in the icy regions of the North Atlantic, whose spirit before translation was expanding into a freer, fuller state.
>
> It was afterwards a source of solace to believe she had been permitted to be thus especially near in thought and prayer during those last solemn and supreme hours of existence.

In the wake of the tragedy, Hester wrote another memoir, this time to her lost husband and recalled an occasion in 1909, when they were joined for tea by Colonel John Weir and Lady Alice Leslie. The conversation turned to ocean voyages and 'the perils of the deep'. A curious coincidence was discussed as the great-grandfather of

Henry Forbes-Julian had travelled the world on long voyages then drowned not far from his Aberdeenshire home. Likewise, Hester Forbes-Julian's Cornish seafaring great-grandfather, Captain Pengelly, had also drowned off the coast almost within sight of land. 'Three years later both the Colonel and Forbes Julian perished on the *Titanic*, while two of Lady Alice Leslie's nieces, the Countess of Rothes and Miss Gladys Cherry, were on the doomed vessel, but were mercifully saved in the boats.'

Henry Forbes Julian did not complete his thirteenth crossing of the Atlantic.

The body of Henry Forbes Julian was never recovered and a committee was formed to fund a memorial tablet in the church where his marriage had been solemnised. A member of the committee informed the widow of the proposal: 'Just as the most enduring claim to the enthusiastic regard of our later generations was to have been one of 'the noble Six Hundred', or to have stood in the red line on the deck of the Birkenhead, so it is wished to commemorate your dear husband's participation in the 'Communion of heroism' of that glorious company on the *Titanic*, whose self-denial called forth the admiration of the whole world.' On the first anniversary of her husband's death, Hester paid her own tribute in a notice in *The Times* with a biblical quote from Corinthians: 'Quit you like men, be strong'.

Henry Forbes Julian had journeyed to America on six occasions but was most reluctant to answer the urgent request of a client and make his thirteenth crossing of the Atlantic. His mood changed noticeably and his widow believed: 'This unexpected summons to leave England seemed... from the first to give him a presage of disaster.'

NOSTRADAMUS:
THE TITANIC'S HOROSCOPE HORROR

'Surely this lesson in astrology suggests the wisdom of shipbuilders choosing dates for launching in conformity with astrological ruling.'

Nostradamus, is credited by his followers with predicting, in coded quatrains, many of the great catastrophic events in history. The sixteenth century French 'prophet', had been taught the secrets of astrology by his grandfather and, according to his devotees, his bleak view of the twentieth century included predictions for the First and Second World Wars, the assassination of President Kennedy and the sinking of *Titanic*:

Did Nostradamus predict the sinking of the Titanic?

> The head cut off the valiant Captain,
> Shall be thrown down before his adversary,
> His body hanged from the ship's antenna,
> Confused they will fly with oars against the wind.

With the benefit of hindsight, not foresight, the verse may be ascribed to the noble death of Captain Smith in the ocean (his

The Titanic's fate was written in the 'stars'.

adversary) when radio messages (the ship's antenna) had failed to summon help in time to save everybody on board, leaving (confused) survivors in the lifeboats resisting the cries for help from those perishing with the 'unsinkable' vessel. The ship's first officer Charles Lightoller presented a similar mystical interpretation of events at the British Inquiry: 'Of course, we know now the extraordinary combination of circumstances that existed at that time which you would not meet again in a 100 years; that they should have existed just on that particular night shows, of course, that everything was against us.' Two weeks after the tragedy, details of the ill-starred horoscope chart of the *Titanic* were revealed by 'Venus-Taurus' the astrologer of *Penny Illustrated*:

> Astrology tells us that if ships are launched when the planets are in certain positions disaster *must* ensue. Now, whether this is so or not, it is a fact that at the time of launching the 'Titanic' the stars *did* presage misfortune and early doom.
>
> The science tells us that if at the moment of launching the moon, or the zodiacal sign of the eastern horizon, or both, are afflicted by the planets Saturn or Mars, trouble and loss will follow to a degree measurable by position and signs. Astrology also gives rules that certain signs govern various parts of a ship, thus showing where trouble may be expected.
>
> Now it is an incontrovertible fact that when the 'Titanic' was being launched, not only were the signs above existent, but every planetary aspect was against her, except that of Venus and Mercury. It is also a fact that the chief afflicting planet governs ice and icebergs, and the positions of the affliction by Saturn and by Herchel (who governs the unexpected in life) are identical with those parts which were so damaged as to cause the collapse and the sinking of the 'Titanic'... The opposition of Herchel to Neptune, the Moon and Venus was a very deadly one for the safety of passengers - Herchel meaning destruction and Neptune loss and grief. The opposition of Jupiter and Saturn, with the ominous signification of the sad fatality of the 'Titanic', foreshadowed also the death of millionaires.
>
> These aspects, at the time of launching, occurring as they did, at a new moon, which also presaged disaster to ships and mortality at sea amongst the leisured classes, only served to empathise the 'Titanic's' ill-fate. This new moon sadly enough foretold the death of a great literary personage by unfortunate disaster, which, in the death of Mr W. T. Stead, has very sadly come to pass.

This fatal hour of launching was consummated by two other astrological happenings, without which, the 'Titanic' might have sailed many voyages, ere the inevitable dramatic tragedy might have occurred.

It was tragic that on the very day selected for her departure the moon should (symbolical of the 'Titanic') have been transiting Herchel. It was a dire misfortune, since Herchel was the moon's great opposing malefic, while, again on the day of foundering, the Sun (protector of life) reached the fatal and exact zodiacal point which, planetary service, completed destruction, and this last aspect occurring without any relieving star or planetary force, except that of Venus and Mercury, which foretold success in wireless messages, bringing relief, and saving women - Mercury signifying messages and transit - Venus, luck.

In this connection it was a sad fatality that both Mr W. T. Stead and Colonel Astor should have elected to travel in the 'Titanic', for looking at the date of their birth and their progressive stars, one sees malefic and destroying planets are marshalled into activity and on the night when the 'Titanic' sank, their malefics combined with those of the vessel in [predicting] exiled life... Surely this lesson in astrology suggests the wisdom of shipbuilders choosing dates for launching in conformity with astrological ruling. In any case, no harm would be done and if the planets speak the truth, a warning would be timely given and great disasters saved by a simple alteration in dates.

WARTIME EXPERIENCES

THE DESTROYER

Out of the night it came, that menace of the seas,
Unmarked by sound and unobserved, its prey of souls to seize;
A pallid shape, dim in the fog, a monster on it came,
And wallowed in the ocean path, its toll of death to claim.

All boasts of modern safeguards, mere affections were;
Inventive minds it mocked and giant ships seemed dwarfs to her.
That mammoth ship, with armour plate, was but a cockleshell,
And when its unseen hand reached out, with ease the giant fell.

And then it laughed; it closed its hand; then watched the work it wrought:
The frenzied screams of dying men, sweet music to it brought.
Unmoved it stood, with eager mein, while fifteen hundred souls
Went struggling down for evermore to rest in watery holes.

Its evil deed accomplished, it drew a conquering breath,
And all about the wreckage, a shadow cast – of Death.
The mightiest of giant ships had just obeyed its nod,
And fifteen hundred souls their final voyage made – to God.

By F.W.R., *Brooklyn Daily Eagle*, 17 April 1912

NED PARFETT

THE TITANIC NEWSBOY

*'On both sides of the Atlantic, newspaper editors
grew hysterical.'*

Newspapers around the globe rushed out special editions to satisfy the demand for updates on the most sensational peacetime disaster of the twentieth century. The editor of the *New York Herald* commented on the international appeal of the story, closing his remarks with unintended black humour:

While the sinking of the White Star line giantess claimed more than 1500 victims from all parts of the world and sent the messenger of grief to millions of hearts on both sides of the Atlantic. In the noble band of martyrs that went to the bottom in the

*Newspapers around the globe rushed
out special editions.*

shattered hulk of the *Titanic* were a score of men and women whose names have been well known in all parts of the world for years, owners of immense fortunes, captains of industry, merchant princes, authors, artists and men prominent in the higher professions. The pomp and ceremony which marked the launching of the monster vessel, the dramatic circumstances surrounding the collision and the superb courage of the passengers were just a few of the things which made the wreck of the *Titanic* a happening which touched the high water mark in tragic events.

By contrast, the editor of the London weekly newspaper, *Penny Illustrated* questioned society's values and criticised the obsession with celebrity in the way the story had been covered:

> On both sides of the Atlantic, newspaper editors grew hysterical… Is it newspaper enterprise, or is it the almighty dollar prevailing? Should we have heard quite so much, day after day, had the *"Titanic"* been an old… tramp with miserable emigrants packed from stem to stern with a sheer impossibility of scraping up £100 between them? We think not… The scream is for the almighty dollar, and not for humanity at all – as witnessing the proportion; two pages and a half for the millionaire and highly placed, and then "sailors, stewardesses and steerage also ran" – or sank.

The most enduring image of publicising the disaster, is a famous photograph portraying a youthful news vendor standing outside the White Star Line offices near Trafalgar Square in Cockspur Street, London. The paperboy is displaying a poster for the *Evening News* with the grim banner headline: '*Titanic* Disaster Great Loss of Life'. The lad has been identified as fifteen-year-old Ned Parfett, whose ultimate fate proved to be as tragic as the loss of the great ship. Six years after this iconic photograph was taken, the former newsboy

Ned Parfett outside the White Star offices in London.

was serving in the British Army when he was killed during a German bombardment just days before the Armistice was declared to end the First World War.

Born in London, Ned was named after his father and was one of four brothers who answered the call to enlist for 'King and Country'. One brother fought in the disastrous campaign in the Dardanelles of 1915, surviving the war to become part of the occupation army in defeated Germany. Another brother avoided becoming a casualty of the bloody battle on the Somme in 1916, only to be wounded and gassed at the third battle of Ypres in Belgium. The third brother also survived the war leaving Ned as the only member of the quartet not to return home. Young Ned enlisted in the Royal Artillery in 1916, first serving as a bicycle dispatch rider before undertaking reconnaissance duties as a signaller in the battery serving under a Forward Observation Officer. In this post he was responsible for relaying messages between battery and brigade on his bicycle. Ned served with distinction during a number of dangerous missions at the Front and his gallant conduct earned him a mention in dispatches and the award of the Military Medal.

On 29 October 1918, Ned Parfett lost his life at the age of twenty-two. Stationed in France, the young soldier was collecting his clothes from the quartermaster's stores in readiness to go home on leave, when a shell scored a direct hit on the military building, killing him and two comrades instantly. Their bodies lay side by side in the British cemetery at Verchain-Maugre. Following the death of Ned, his elder brother Gunner George Parfett, wrote from his own post in Belgium to the Headquarters of the 29th Brigade, Royal Field Artillery, enquiring for details about the fate of his sibling. In due course, he received a reply from 2nd Lieutenant Percy Hunt, the officer who had instigated recognition of Ned's conspicuous bravery:

> Referring to your enquiry about your brother's death, I much regret to inform you he was killed when the Brigade was near Verchain, near which place he was buried. At the time of his death he was in the Q.M. [Quarter Master's] Stores and a shell fell on the stores, killing him outright. …
>
> I wish to inform you how highly we valued his services, and I recommended him for his Military Medal which in every way he had won. On many occasions he accompanied me during severe shelling and I always placed the utmost confidence in him.

JOHN PRIEST
JONAH OF THE HIGH SEAS

*'He has seen four of the vessels in which he was serving sink,
and three others have been damaged.'*

Maritime incidents and shipwrecks were a recurring occupational hazard to three surviving members of the *Titanic* crew: stewardess Violet Jessop, lookout Archie Jewell and fireman John Priest. Before joining the *Titanic* for her maiden voyage, Jessop and Priest were onboard the White Star liner the *Olympic*, also captained by the ill-fated Edward Smith, and which collided with *HMS Hawke* in 1911.

During the First World War, all three White Star employees served on the *Titanic*'s sister ships *Olympic* and

Shipwrecks were a occupational hazard for 'Jonah' Priest.

Britannic. The latter was requisitioned as a hospital ship transporting sick and wounded soldiers from the Middle East to Britain. Under the command of Captain Charles Bartlett, *Britannic* completed several successful missions in the Mediterranean before she struck a mine in November 1916 and sank in less than an hour. Fortunately, the vessel was not carrying any patients and only thirty members of the 1,125 crew and medical staff lost their lives. The Germans claimed that the hospital ship had been targeted by a U-Boat because she was being used as a troop carrier, but this was later shown to be false when the log of the enemy submarine involved showed that it had laid mines in the area and had not fired on the ship. Royal Navy destroyers picked up the survivors from the *Britannic* who included Violet Jessop, Archie Jewell and John Priest.

The *Britannic* was the largest vessel lost in the First World War. Violet Jessop later described the final death-roll in her memoirs: 'She dipped her head a little, then a little lower and still lower. All the deck machinery fell into the sea like child's toys. Then she took a fearful plunge, her stern rearing hundreds of feet into the air, until with a final roar, she disappeared into the depths, the noise of her going resounding through the water with undreamt of violence.' The wartime nurse's ordeal was not yet over, for, she suffered a fractured skull and a badly gashed leg when the lifeboat she joined was sucked into the main propeller of the sinking ship. Violet was one of the fortunate ones – many of her fellow crew members were killed in the incident and the sea was strewn with mutilated bodies.

Having survived the loss of the *Titanic* and *Britannic*, it was third time unlucky for able seaman Archie Jewell when he transferred to the hospital ship *Donegal*. In April 1917 the ship was torpedoed by a German submarine and sank in the English Channel. Twenty-eight-year-old Archie lost his life along with ten other crew members. Amazingly, one of the survivors of the tragedy was the unsinkable John Priest who escaped with a severe head injury. The *Britannic* and *Donegal* were just two of the doomed wartime vessels in which John Priest served. The able seaman was also wounded when the *Alcantara* was torpedoed by the German cruiser *Greif* in February 1916. The shipwreck-prone seaman had transferred to the *Titanic* from the *Asturias* which was involved in an accident on her maiden voyage and subsequently had her stern blown off by a torpedo causing the loss of thirty-five lives in March 1917. John Priest passed away on land aged only forty-eight following a bout of pneumonia in 1937. Apparently, he had felt compelled to give up his adventurous seafaring career when superstitious sailors made it quite clear that they viewed him as an unsuitable shipmate. His reputation as a modern day 'Jonah' was publicised in an article published in *The Times* in April 1917:

> John Priest, who lives in Southampton, is only 29 years of age. He has been on the sea since his youth, and has served in many waters.
>
> He has seen four of the vessels in which he was serving sink, and three others have been damaged.
>
> Several years ago he was in the '*Asturias*' when she met with an accident on her maiden voyage. He was one of the survivors of the disaster which overtook the '*Titanic*' on her maiden voyage five years ago, escaping with frost-bitten toes and an injured leg.
>
> He was also in the '*Olympic*' when that vessel and the '*Hawke*' came into collision near the Isle of Wight some years ago, and he served in the '*Alcantra*' during her gallant fight with the German raider '*Greif*' in the North Sea.
>
> The '*Alcantra*' was sunk by a torpedo and Priest was wounded by shrapnel during the fight.
>
> Later he joined the '*Britannic*', and was serving in that ship when she sank last November. His last ship was the '*Donegal*' from which he escaped with a rather serious injury to his head.

EDITH PEARS

WARTIME LOSS AND THE VICTORIA CROSS

*'Second Lieut. Wearne... ran along the top of the trench,
firing and throwing bombs.'*

Tom Pears, an executive of his family's well-known soap manu-
facturing company, lost his life on the *Titanic*, while his wife of
two years survived the disaster. During the First World War, widow
Edith Pears, maiden name Wearne, served as a nurse driving an
ambulance for the British Red Cross before joining the Women's
Royal Naval Service (WRNS) attached as a driver chauffeuring
naval officers to and from the Admiralty in London. While sharing
a flat with Norah Crowe, she began a romance with her friend's
brother, an electrician whose poor eyesight had exempted him from
military service. At the war's end Douglas Crowe and Edith Pears
were married and settled on a tea plantation in India.

Edith's wartime romance and her new found happiness was
marred by the terrible price paid by her three brothers, Keith, Frank
and Geoffrey who served with tragic consequence on the Western
Front. The only one of the three to survive the conflict was youngest
brother, Geoffrey, who fought with the Canadian Army in the
trenches. The constant bombardment led him to suffer shellshock
which drove him insane and, after being demobbed in 1919, he was
committed to a mental institution where he spent the remaining
fifty-eight years of his life. Eldest brother, Captain Keith Wearne,
was a regular soldier who joined the Essex Regiment from

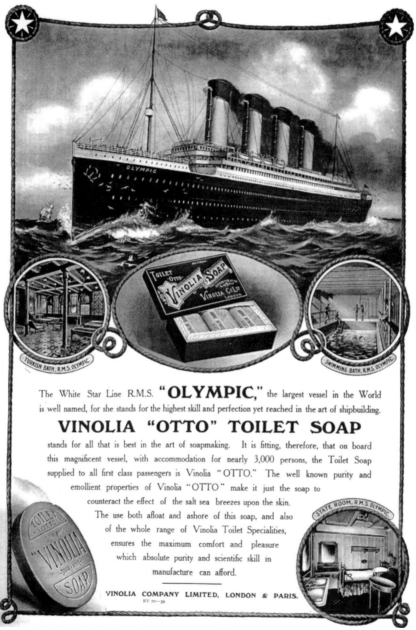

The White Star Line's choice of soap was a rival of Pears.

Sandhurst. He was killed in action in May 1917, coincidentally, the same month that his sibling Frank Wearne returned to active service having recovered from appalling wounds suffered at the Battle of the Somme ten months earlier in July 1916. With no time to get over the bereavement of his brother, the young officer rejoined the 11th Battalion of the Essex Regiment based near the town of Lens in Northern France. Two months later he took part in a raid across No Man's Land. The aim was to capture a section of the enemy trenches, destroy dugouts and underground tunnels, then bring prisoners back for questioning in a dangerous 'mop-up' operation. Subalterns had the shortest life expectancy of any infantry soldiers as they were expected to lead by example. Second Lieutenant Frank Wearne fully realised that the mission would probably bring about his death. The plan, though ultimately carried out successfully, resulted in half of the attacking force subsequently becoming casualties.

Split into three raiding parties, one commanded by Wearne, a counter-attack by the enemy soldiers threatened to destroy the mission until an act of the utmost daring and bravery by Wearne rectified the situation. Leaping on to the parapet of an enemy trench, he courageously fired his revolver and threw grenades exposing himself to a hail of bullets from rifles and machine guns. His troops were inspired to follow his example and the ferocity of the charge caused the Germans to fall back. However, Wearne's gallant action cost him his life and he was posthumously awarded the

Frank Bernard Wearne VC.

Victoria Cross. *The London Gazette* published the citation to Second Lieutenant Frank Bernard Wearne:

> For most conspicuous bravery when in command of a small party on the left of a raid on the enemy's trenches. He gained his objective in the face of much opposition, and by his magnificent example and daring was able to maintain this position for a considerable time, according to instructions. During this period Second Lieut. Wearne and his small party were repeatedly counter-attacked. Grasping the fact that if the left flank was lost his men would have to give way, Second Lieut. Wearne, at a moment when the enemy's attack was being heavily pressed and when matters were most critical, leapt on the parapet, and, followed by his left section, ran along the top of the trench, firing and throwing bombs. This unexpected and daring manoeuvre threw the enemy off his guard and back in disorder. Whilst on top of the trench Second Lieut. Wearne was severely wounded, but refused to leave his men. Afterwards he remained in the trench directing operations, consolidating his position and encouraging all ranks. Just before the order to withdraw was given, this gallant officer was again severely hit for the second time, and while being carried away was mortally wounded. By his tenacity in remaining at his post, though severely wounded, and by his magnificent fighting spirit, he was enabled to hold on to his flank.

JOHN HUME

THE VIOLINIST AND THE MUTILATED NURSE

'A man here has had his head cut off. My breast taken away.'

As the lifeboats left the stricken vessel, the survivors were entertained by the ship's band. All eight musicians on board perished including John 'Jock' Hume of Dumfries. The twenty-one -year-old violinist left behind a pregnant fiancée, Mary Costin, who, when her daughter, Johnann was born, applied for a grant from the welfare fund set up to help the families of

Titanic victims and was awarded £67. However, the money was sent to Andrew Hume, John's father, who rejected the grandchild conceived outside marriage and refused to handover the money, forcing the single-mother to take him to court to recover the compensation that was judged to be rightfully hers. Tragically, Johnann lost her remaining parent when Mary died of tuberculosis in 1922.

Within weeks of the outbreak of the First World War in 1914, Andrew

Violinist John Hume.

Hume suffered another blow when his youngest daughter Kate, produced letters declaring that her elder sister Grace had been tortured to death while serving as a wartime nurse in Belgium. According to Kate, the letters had been personally delivered by a colleague of Grace, Nurse Mullard, who wrote:

> Grace requested me to tell you that her last thoughts were of… you, and that you are not to worry about her. She would be going to meet her Jock. Those were her last words. She endured great agony in her last hours.
>
> One of the soldiers (our men) caught two German soldiers in the act of cutting off her left breast, her right one having already been cut off. They were killed instantly by our soldiers. Grace managed to scrawl this enclosed note before I found her, but we all say your sister was a heroine.
>
> Dear Kate, This is to say goodbye. I have not long to live. The hospital has been set on fire. Germans cruel. A man here has had his head cut off. My breast taken away… Goodbye, Grace.

A heartbroken Andrew Hume immediately contacted the War Office requesting further details about the report and was then stunned to receive a telegram from his supposedly dead daughter Grace: 'Reports untrue. Safe in Huddersfield'. She followed it up with a letter to her father condemning the reports as 'an absolute mystery to me. I never heard of such a person as Nurse Mullard. I hope the police will take it up.'

A police investigation did take place and they soon discovered that a cruel hoax had been perpetrated by seventeen-year-old clerk Kate Hume, who was indicted for forging letters. Medical experts expressed the opinion that the prisoner was in a state of 'adolescent hysteria' that had conjured up in her mind vivid images which she could not differentiate from the truth. When the accused testified in her own defence, it emerged that her mother had died after a long illness. Her father had subsequently remarried, but, she did not get on with her stepmother, causing her to leave home and move into lodgings. She was in a depressed state and, after reading a great deal about the enemy's barbaric treatment of women, she was convinced that her sister had been killed at the Front:

> I had no intention of causing any sensation or alarming my father, stepmother or anybody else. I do not know why I wrote it, but I fancied what I said would be the way Grace would have written of herself in her last minutes. I could fancy the whole thing happening as it was written, but I had no idea that anybody would see the letters.
>
> I cannot say what made me do it, except the cruelties the Germans were committing. I was seeing and imagining the things I wrote. I cannot think why I wrote the name Mullard, except that I believed a man of that name went down on the *Titanic*, and perhaps it got into my head, which at the time seemed to be turning around.
>
> I firmly believed what was in the letters was true and that Grace had been killed. I had worked myself into that belief. I did not think I was doing anything improper.

The family's nightmare, played out in a blaze of embarrassing publicity, came to an end when the jury pronounced a verdict of 'guilty' with a recommendation of leniency and Kate Hume was immediately released as she had already been held in custody for three months while awaiting trial in the notorious case of 'The Mutilated Nurse'.

CHARLES LIGHTOLLER
A LIFE ON THE OCEAN WAVE

'If he can survive the Titanic, he can survive anything.'

Christian Scientist Charles Lightoller was Second Officer on the *Titanic* in the terrifying crisis when, by thinking of the words of the 91st Psalm: 'He shall give his angels charge over thee,' his religious beliefs sustained him as the ship plunged to the bottom of the ocean. As the sea swamped the deck he launched the only remaining lifeboat, a flat bottomed collapsible, then dived overboard at the last moment and clambered aboard the light craft that had overturned in the wash, but stayed afloat upside down and carried him and thirty others to safety.

By the age of twenty-four, Lightoller had already survived one shipwreck, a fire at sea and a cyclone serving on windjammers, and almost died from a bout of malaria upon transferring to steamships. Temporarily leaving the sea, he briefly led an adventurous life, gold prospecting, cow punching and riding the rails as a hobo in North America, before returning to England and resumed his seafaring career in 1900, sailing the Atlantic with the White Star Line.

Two years after his ordeal on the *Titanic*, war was declared and Lightoller became a lieutenant in the Royal Navy serving on former White Star liner *Oceanic* which had been converted into an armed merchant cruiser. While patrolling the Shetland Isles, the vessel ran aground and the crew were forced to abandon ship which later broke up in a storm in September 1914. Given command of a torpedo boat, Lightoller was awarded the Distinguished Service

An overturned collapsible lifeboat carried Lightoller to safety.

Cross (DSC) for successfully attacking a German Zeppelin in July 1916, and promoted to commander of the torpedo-boat-destroyer *Falcon*. In April 1918, as Lightoller was lying in his bunk, the *Falcon* embarrassingly collided with a trawler and sank on the sixth anniversary of the *Titanic* disaster. Quickly restoring his damaged reputation, Lightoller won praise three months later after taking command of the destroyer *Garry*. In July 1918, he gave the order to ram and sink the German submarine UB110. For this action,

Lightoller was awarded a bar to his DSC and ended the war as a full Commander in the Royal Navy.

Returning to civilian life, Lightoller resigned after spending over twenty years in the service of the White Star Line. Making money from property speculation and running a guest house with his wife, he continued to enjoy what appeared at first to be a more leisurely life at sea in his motor cruiser *Sundowner*. Then, prior to the outset of the Second World War in 1939, the Lightollers posed as an elderly couple on a cruise, conducting espionage and surveying the German coastline for the Royal Navy. The retired sixty-six-year-old officer was called into action once again, sailing with the flotilla of small boats that crossed the English Channel and ran the gauntlet of enemy fire to evacuate over 330,000 marooned soldiers from Dunkirk on the French coast. The *Sundowner* crewed by Lightoller and one of his three sons, Roger, succeeded in rescuing 130 troops in the historic mission carried out in 1940. The skipper was totally unaware until the operation was over that among the soldiers waiting on the beach was his eldest son, Lieutenant Colonel Richard Lightoller. Tragically, he was the only one of the three brothers to survive the war. Charles Lightoller's youngest son, Brian, an RAF pilot, was killed early in the war during a bombing raid over Whillhemshaven, whereas Roger went on to join the Royal Navy where he commanded motor gun boats. He was mentioned in despatches and awarded the DSC before losing his life during the last month of the war in a raid by enemy commandoes in Northern France.

Commander Charles Lightoller served in the Home Guard and was also engaged by the Royal Navy ferrying small vessels until the end of hostilities. During his heroics at Dunkirk, it was said that when one of the rescued soldiers heard that the skipper of the *Sundowner* had been an officer on the *Titanic,* he was tempted to jump overboard and wait for another boat. However, he quickly changed his mind when one of his pals pointed out, 'If he can survive the *Titanic,* he can survive anything.'

SOS: STORIES OF SUICIDE

MASTER AND MAN

The Captain stood where a Captain should
For the Law of the Sea is grim;
The Owner romped while the ship was swamped
And no law bothered him.

The Captain stood where the Captain should
When a Captain's ship goes down
But the Owner led when the women fled,
For an Owner must not drown.

The Captain sank as a man of Rank,
While his Owner turned away;
The Captain's grave was his bridge and brave,
He earned his seaman's pay.

To hold your place in the ghastly face
of Death on the Sea at Night
Is a Seaman's job, but to flee with the mob
Is an Owner's Noble Right.

Ben Hecht, *Chicago Journal*, 17 June 1912

THE COWARD OF THE TITANIC

'What kind of man do you think I am?'

Cornish emigrant Ada West recorded in a diary how she and her two young daughters were helped into one of the first lifeboats by her husband Arthur, before he dashed back to their cabin to fetch some hot milk for his family. When he returned, the boat was being lowered into the sea, so he shimmied down a rope and handed them the thermos flask before climbing back on to the deck. Although Arthur West clearly had the opportunity to remain in the boat, he passed up the chance, nobly observing the rule of the sea 'women and children first'. However, as he waited chivalrously for imminent death, two other men, jumped into the same lifeboat. According to Mrs West, they 'concealed themselves under the ladies' skirts and had to be asked to stop lighting cigarettes as there was a danger of the dresses becoming ignited'.

One of the stowaways who leapt into the lifeboat while the officers weren't looking was Japanese civil servant Masabumi Hosono who, in a letter to his wife, explained, 'I tried to prepare myself for the last moment with no agitation, making up my mind not to leave anything disgraceful as a Japanese.' However, Hosono added that he then made a decision not to 'share the same destiny as the *Titanic*' - a sentiment that was greeted with disgust in his homeland where he was vilified for his actions. It transpired that he had been turned back from the lifeboats three times before sneaking past the officers. In a culture imbrued with the courageous code of

Bruce Ismay was castigated for not going down with his ship.

the Samurai, his survival at the expense of others was branded cowardly and he was urged to do the honourable thing and commit 'harakiri'. Unrepentant, the shamed survivor responded to the criticism by simply asserting, 'I'm alive here and now, what's wrong with that?'

The Chairman and Managing Director of the White Star Line, Bruce Ismay, was another person who never lived down the fact that he had deserted the ship, for which he had ultimate responsibility for sending to sea with an inadequate number of lifeboats. The town of Ismay in Jackson County, Texas was so ashamed of the ignominy associated with the name that they promptly changed it. Savaged by critics in the American and British press, he was dubbed 'Brute Ismay' and 'The Coward of the *Titanic*'.

Future Oscar-winning film screenwriter Ben Hecht, then a young newspaperman in Chicago, wrote a scathing poem contrasting the actions of Captain Smith and Bruce Ismay. An extract reads: 'The captain stood where the captain should, when a captain's ship goes down; but the owner led when the women fled, for an owner must not drown.' Even in that most English of magazines *John Bull*, the editor published an open letter to Ismay posing a pertinent question: 'How is it that *you*, above all people, were in one of the lifeboats?... Your place was at the captain's side till every man, woman and child was safely off the ship'. Ismay answered the mounting criticism in a statement to the press: 'What kind of man do you think I am? Certainly there were no women and children around. I thought they had all been saved. I think it was the last boat that was lowered I went into. I did then what any other passenger would do. And tell me how I was different from any other passenger? I was not running the ship. If they say I was president of the company that owns the ship then I want to know where you will draw the line.'

In the beleaguered shipping magnate's hometown of Liverpool, a false rumour spread that, unable to stand the strain no more, he had finally listened to his conscience and done the decent thing by committing suicide. An 'old friend' of Ismay, shocked at this scurrilous suggestion, immediately dashed off a letter of protest to the editor of *The Times*: 'At a moment of such deep tragedy and sorrow for Mr Ismay and his friends it seems incredible that he should be censured for doing what other men rightly did by accepting the last chance of saving his life after he had done everything in his power for others, it is unworthy of the traditions of a great country, that such criticism should be heard, and at such a sad moment.' Ismay was cleared by the subsequent British Inquiry, presided over by Lord Mersey, who found that he was under no obligation to go down with the ship. Furthermore, in his lordship's opinion it would have been a futile gesture: 'Had he not jumped in [the lifeboat], he would have merely added one more life, namely his own, to the numbers of those lost.'

DR HENRY FRAUENTHAL
PREY TO DEATH

'It seemed as all the devils of hell had been let loose.'

Titanic survivor, Dr Henry Frauenthal, revealed in an interview with the press that his conscience was troubling him with the terrible realisation that so many men and women had been abandoned to their fate on the stricken liner:

> When the word came that we were sinking and the lifeboats were ordered over the side, the panic was fearful. From all sides came shrieks and groans and cries, and it seemed as all the devils of hell had been let loose.
>
> Just now I am so thankful to be alive that my appreciation of the horror is dulled. I am only afraid that when I recover from the first shock it will all come back to me again, and I would rather have gone down with the boat, I think, than have to live over again, even in my imagination, the last few minutes of that dreadful night.
>
> I would rather have stayed, too, than know that women went down with the *Titanic*, but I swear we thought every woman on the ship had been placed safely in the boats. It was 'Women first' with all of the men, and at last it seemed as if the decks had been cleared of them, for not one was to be seen save those already lowered.
>
> Then the officers ordered the men to leave the sinking vessel and we left for the boats, not knowing, any one of us,

Many people were left behind as 'prey to death'.

I think, how many of our fellow men we were leaving behind
as prey to death.

The New York physician had, in fact, seen his wife safely take a
seat into a lifeboat, then accompanied by his brother Isaac, joined
her by suddenly leaping in when the ship's officers were distracted
lowering the boat over the side. Although, the craft was only two-
thirds full, the doctor's considerable bulk landed on top of unwary

The doctor jumped in as a lifeboat was lowered.

passenger Annie Stengel, rendering her unconscious and breaking two of her ribs. Henry and his wife Clara were honeymooners, having married at Nice in France nearly three weeks earlier. Upon reaching dry land on the *Carpathia*, the forty-nine-year-old orthopaedic specialist wasted no time in returning to the Hospital for Deformities and Joint Diseases that he had founded seven years earlier. It was announced that sixty crippled patients who had prayed for the newlyweds safe deliverance would be taken in their wheelchairs to the verandas to look out for their approach, then greet the couple with cheers and the waving of handkerchiefs before holding an informal reception.

Dr Frauenthal continued to expand his successful private practice from a two-room clinic to the largest institution of its kind in the world. Having married late in life, he and his wife raised a foster child, Natalie, before the couple both began to suffer from mental heath issues. In the early hours of the morning, a few days before his sixty-fifth birthday in March 1927, Dr Frauenthal jumped from the seventh-floor bedroom window of his apartment. Laying dead on the ground with a crushed skull, his body was discovered by the night nurse after she visited his room and found his bed empty at 7am. Frauenthal's widow was too ill to be told the bad news. Chief Medical Examiner Charles Norris attributed the death to a fall from the window 'due to mental derangement' which had been brought on by overwork and failing health. Medical colleagues revealed that the medical innovator had been in a serious 'nervous state' for some time and had not operated on patients for two years due to his incapacity.

Bequeathing most of his $300,000 fortune to the hospital that had been his life's work, Dr Frauenthal added a bizarre twist to his will, requesting that his ashes should be held in a vault and scattered from the hospital rooftop on the fiftieth anniversary of its incorporation in 1955.

GEORGE BRERETON
DEATH OF A CONMAN

'It was hard to row, for nearly every stroke hit a body.'

The *New York Herald* reported a week after the sinking that, when the *Titanic* crashed at full speed, 'The men in the smoking room who were deep in their game of cards – sent one of their number to the window to report on what had happened. He stuck his poker

A gambler remarked that the ship had 'only grazed an iceberg'.

hand of cards into the side pocket of his coat, gazed out of the window and remarked that she "had only grazed an iceberg". Then the enthusiasts went on with their game, but it was not for long. The game was never finished and most of those who were in it never will play another.'

However, one survivor from the First Class smoking room, was a cardsharp known in criminal circles as George 'Boy' Bradley, real name George Brereton, who was travelling on the liner using the alias George Brayton. Taking a break from the card game where he had been stalking a potential victim, 'Brayton' was strolling on deck when the ship lurched to a halt. When the last lifeboat had left and the vessel was in its death throes, 'Brayton' grabbed a life preserver and jumped overboard: 'I was in the water two hours,' he told the press. 'I was finally picked up by a lifeboat containing twenty-two passengers. When I got on board I took an oar, but it was hard to row, for nearly every stroke hit a body.'

The unscrupulous conman and professional gambler quickly got over his brush with death. He continued his work after being rescued by the *Carpathia*, attempting to set up fellow survivor Charles Stengel for a horse racing scam. Meeting up several weeks later at a New York hotel, Brereton introduced Stengel to his 'brother-in-law' called MacDonald, allegedly a superintendent with Western Union. 'Big Mac' explained that he could arrange for the telegraphing of horse racing results to be delayed for eight minutes, presenting a window of opportunity to bet on the declared winner. Stengel could buy into the deal by donating $1000 to the betting pool. Instead of meekly handing over the money, the honest businessman flew at the two crooks with fists flailing. After pleading with him not to 'squeal' the two crooks fled when the police were called.

A similar ruse led to Brereton's downfall in 1933. While a member of a notorious band of scam artists known as the 'Maybury Gang', he was arrested with an accomplice in Yosemite National Park - accused of swindling $27,000 from a retired businessman who was also led to believe he was placing a bet on a 'sure thing' in what proved to be a fake horse race supposedly taking place in Omaha. Following a period of incarceration for this episode, George apparently went straight and became a car salesman sharing a home with his younger sister, Emily Lathrop, in Los Angeles.

The crooked gambler's family was seemingly dogged by bad luck. When news of the *Titanic* disaster reached New York, someone calling himself C.J.E. Clayton, residing at the Hotel Prince George, read the latest bulletins and collapsed on the pavement. Someone in the crowd of spectators who gathered around the prostrate man on the pavement, summoned the attention of two policemen to the man's condition. As the patrolmen approached the man, he moaned: 'My God, my two brothers and my little daughter were on that ship [although no-one named Clayton appeared in the passenger list]. And I lost my wife and other child in the [1906] San Francisco earthquake. I had been waiting seven years for the return of my little girl and brothers.'

When the man recovered from his fainting spell, he claimed to be the 'brother-in-law' of survivor 'George Brayton'. In the circumstances, there's a strong possibility that 'Mr Clayton' had an accomplice picking the pockets of passers-by who had gathered round. Nevertheless, real tragedy occurred in George Brereton's personal life. In 1922, his son had died following a tonsillectomy operation and, overcome by grief, his wife Grace committed suicide by shooting herself at their home in Los Angeles. In July 1942, on the twentieth anniversary of his wife's death, in the same dwelling, the depressed sixty-seven-year-old ended his life in similar fashion. With a twelve gauge shotgun pointed to his head, George Brereton pulled the trigger and blew his brains out.

WASHINGTON DODGE
A MATTER OF HONOUR

'The assault upon his good name overcame him.'

Captain Edward Smith was lauded by many passengers as a heroic figure, portrayed as going down with his ship shouting through a megaphone urging those around him to die with dignity and 'Be British'. Furthermore, a dramatic story emerged of how the fearless skipper swam to rescue a baby that was floating in the water on a mass of wreckage. According to one eye-witness, gambler George Brayton, Captain Smith grasped the child, struck out for a lifeboat, handed the infant over to an officer, then, bravely refused to save himself by climbing aboard and sank beneath the waves near the stern of his ship.

Captain Smith gave the rallying cry 'Be British'.

In total contrast, many survivors alleged that Captain Smith had committed suicide. Grechen Longley of New York, told the press: 'Captain Smith made two attempts to kill himself and at last he succeeded. He was in his library when the officers saw him with a revolver in his hand. They rushed their superior officer and tore the gun from him. The captain struggled with them desperately, broke away, and rushed to the bridge, where he killed himself, placing the revolver in his mouth and firing.'

Witnesses claimed the captain had rescued a baby.

Yet, another unsubstantiated version of events concerning the death of Captain Smith was told by Mrs Washington Dodge of San Francisco :

> I saw a man who I am sure was Captain Smith. He was being pushed onto a life raft. He flung his arms about and struggled like a mad man. It was easy to see he did not want to go. But the men who pushed him insisted and at length they got him onto the raft. He looked wildly about for a moment, waving his arms in despair and supplication. Then he leapt off the raft into the ice-caked sea which closed over his head forever. A woman in my boat moaned and fainted when she saw the captain take his life and I felt sick at heart for I thought of my absent husband... When I saw that ship go down I asked God to help me for my son's sake to be brave. I thought my husband had gone down too.

Ruth Dodge was relieved to be reunited with her husband on board the *Carpathia* although, the story did not have a happy ending. Seven years later, former physician, politician and banker Washington Dodge became embroiled in a lawsuit. He was sued by two investors who claimed they had been misled when Dodge recommended that they should buy shares in a wireless company he was associated with, knowing it had insoluble financial problems. The case preyed on the mind of Dr Dodge severely effecting his health. In June 1919, Mrs. Dodge organised a family trip to Santa Barbara where her ailing husband might recuperate. On the day they were due to travel, she left their apartment to do some last minute shopping. When she returned, she made the horrific discovery that her husband had shot himself. Dodge had taken the elevator to the garage basement armed with a pistol and fired it at his forehead. The bullet fractured his skull and drove fragments of bone deep into the tissues of the brain. The victim suffered a second fracture when he fell and struck his head on the concrete floor. Still alive, but weak through loss of blood, the wounded man staggered to the elevator and pressed the button to take him back to the lobby where his plight was spotted by the porter. Semi-conscious and incoherent, Washington Dodge was rushed to hospital, but nothing could be done to save him and he died nine days later. His personal physician told the press 'Dr Dodge has been ill more than a year. A month ago the illness became much more severe, and with it developed a bad mental state'. The dead man's attorney confirmed the pending legal action, claiming damages of over $50,000, though totally without foundation, was the sole reason why his sixty-year-old client had taken his own life, mistakenly believing the matter reflected on his honour: 'Dr Dodge cared nothing about the financial side of the suit, but the assault upon his good name overcame him. He collapsed under the strain and was suffering from temporary insanity.'

However, it transpired that another law suit was under consideration by the stockholder's committee of the company. They had discovered that when Dodge had transferred the rights of the company to the government, he had received a commission of $115,000 to which, he was not legally entitled. Even as the former president of the company lay dying, the stockholder's legal representative announced his intention to recover the money stating: 'Washington Dodge, in my judgement, is not entitled to a single cent.'

FREDERICK FLEET
LOOKOUT FOR DANGER

'I am in deep trouble.'

Lookout Frederick Fleet was the first person on the *Titanic* to spot the iceberg that sent her to the bottom of the ocean. Despite receiving warnings of ice in the area, Captain Smith, chose not to give the order for the vessel to reduce speed. Perched high above the deck in the crow's nest with fellow seaman Reginald Lee, the two men were simply told by Quartermaster Robert Hichens to keep a 'sharp lookout' for 'small ice', completely unaware that they were speeding straight towards an iceberg that was protruding over eighty feet above the water. The two men were not provided with binoculars which had been mysteriously missing from the 'nest' since the new ship had completed her trial run from Belfast to South-

Lookout Frederick Fleet was the first man to spot the iceberg.

ampton. In Fleet and Lee's opinion, if eyeglasses had been available on such a clear starlit night, with no swell on a calm sea, the iceberg would have been seen in good time, allowing appropriate action to be taken to avoid the forthcoming disaster. At a Court of Inquiry in London, Lee testified that there was a haze on the horizon and his shipmate commented: 'If we can see through this we will be lucky.'

Asked by counsel whether the haze was very bad, Lee retorted sardonically, 'It was so bad that you could not see an iceberg through it.' Fleet gave evidence that shortly before his two-hour watch was due to end, he saw a black mass less than half a mile in the distance and immediately sounded the alarm, alerting the bridge of the looming danger. The warning came too late to take sufficient evasive action. At the helm was Robert Hichens who told the press upon his arrival in New York:

> I took the wheel at ten o'clock, and Mr Murdoch, the first officer, took the watch. It was twenty minutes to twelve and I was steering when there were three gongs from the lookout, which indicated that some object was ahead. Almost instantly, it could not have been more than four or five seconds, when the lookout man called down on the telephone, 'Iceberg ahead!' Hardly had the words come to me when there was a crash… There was a light grating on the port bow, then a heavy crash on the starboard side. I could hear the engines stop, and the lever closing the water tight emergency doors… The *Titanic* listed, perhaps five degrees, to the starboard, and then began to the settle in the water.

Contradicting this statement of events by Robert Hichens was First Class Steward Thomas Whiteley. He gave an interview alleging that William Murdoch had committed suicide after ignoring warnings about the iceberg for twenty-five minutes. According to Whiteley, he had talked to the two lookout men and one of them told him: 'From the crow's nest we sighted the iceburg that hit us at 11.15. I at once reported it to Mr. Murdoch. It was not white but a sort of bluish colour plainly distinguishable against the clear sky. Twice afterward I reported the iceberg to Mr. Murdoch. I could not see that he at all varied the *Titanic*'s course. He knew he should have changed his course. He shot himself because he knew it'.

Having made for the lifeboats and survived the sinking, tragic fates awaited Frederick Fleet and Reginald Lee. Sixteen moths later, Lee sadly died aged forty-three, having contracted pneumonia. The experience of the disaster did not deter Fleet from continuing a career at sea for another twenty-four years. Once ashore, in the economic depression of the mid 1930s, he obtained work firstly for Harland and Wolff, the shipbuilding firm that had constructed the *Titanic*, then became the shore master-at-arms for the Union Castle Steamship Company. In retirement, he spent his later years as a part-time street corner newspaper vendor, selling copies of the local newspaper, the *Southampton Echo*. He made headlines himself early in January 1965, when the newspaper announced that their former employee had committed suicide. The former seaman was found hanging from the post of a clothes line in the garden of his home. The seventy-six-year-old pensioner had been extremely depressed since losing his wife Eva who had died over the Christmas period. The elderly widower's state of mind deteriorated further when he was callously given notice by his landlord – his wife's brother, Philip LeGros, who subsequently found the body of his relative and former lodger. In a letter to a friend written shortly before his death, Fleet wrote: 'Just a few lines to let you know I am in deep trouble. I have lost my wife, also I am leaving my house, the place where I have been living. There is only my brother-in-law and myself, we cannot agree.'

Amongst Frederick Fleet's affects preserved for posterity was his seaman's discharge book in which his *Titanic* experience is recorded in two terse sentences, 'Discharged at sea. Destination intended for New York'.

JACK THAYER
A SKETCHY MEMORY

'We could see groups of the almost fifteen hundred people aboard, clinging in clusters or bunches, like swarming bees; only to fall in masses.'

Seventeen-year-old Jack Thayer junior, was separated from his parents as they made for the boat decks and told the press about his amazing escape from the *Titanic*: 'People began jumping from the stern. I thought of jumping myself, but was afraid of being stunned when hitting the water. Finally, I jumped out feet first... I was sucked down and as I came up my hands touched the cork fender of an overturned boat. I looked up and saw some men on the top and asked them to give me a hand. In a short time the bottom was covered with about twenty-five or thirty men... We had the second officer, Mr Lightoller, on board. He had an officer's whistle and whistled for the boat in the distance to come up and take us off. It took about an hour and a half for the boats to draw near.'

Jack Thayer junior.

The stranded survivors were rescued from their precarious position on the capsized collapsible boat and distributed to other lifeboats. Among them was the very last lifeboat to be successfully launched which contained able seaman William A. Lucas. He had been transferred from the *Olympic* to the *Titanic* and boarded only fifteen minutes before sailing. Off duty and playing a quiet game of 'nap' on the night the ship was wrecked, he escaped at the last moment when the water was up to the bridge and he boarded a collapsible which 'floated off' the flooded deck. Surviving the ordeal, the sailor's behaviour thereafter was considered 'peculiar' although he continued his naval career serving on several ships including the *Derwent River*, *War Mehtar*, *Polynesia*, *Bellagio* and the *Constance*. After returning from yet another voyage in September 1921, the thirty-five-year-old boarded the Leeds to London train. During the journey, he was found unconscious in a third class compartment having shot himself in the right temple. When the train arrived at King's Cross, the wounded man was taken to the Royal Free Hospital, where he died the following day. Dressed in seaman's uniform, a large sum of money including foreign currency was found on his person, together with a suicide note expressing the wish to leave all his possessions 'to my dear sister'.

Taken aboard the *Carpathia*, Jack Thayer was reunited with his mother Marian and later discovered that his father, Jack Thayer

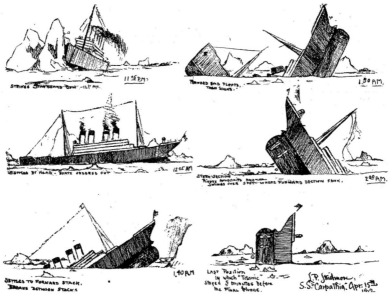

Thayer's sketches of the Titanic's last moments.

senior, a vice-president of the Pennsylvania Railroad, was one of the doomed people whom he saw dying from his vantage point on the upturned lifeboat: 'We could see groups of the almost fifteen hundred people aboard, clinging in clusters or bunches, like swarming bees; only to fall in masses, pairs or singly, as the great part of the ship, two hundred and fifty feet of it, rose into the sky, till it reached a sixty-five or seventy degree angle. Here it seemed to pause, and just hung, for what felt like minutes. Gradually she turned her deck away from us, as though to hide from our sight the awful spectacle'. Despite his youth and the horrifying experience he had endured, Jack Thayer's lucid observations proved to be among the most reliable of the conflicting accounts made by traumatised survivors. In addition, assisted by a passenger on the *Carpathia*, L. P. Skidmore, the teenager produced accurate sketches of the stricken ship's final moments. It controversially depicted his belief that the vessel had broken in two – a contention that was denied by other eye-witnesses but proved to be correct when a salvage team eventually discovered the wreck in 1985.

Jack Thayer served as a captain of artillery during the First World War, then having graduated from university he went into banking and was later appointed Financial Vice-President and Treasurer at the University of Pennsylvania. In 1940, he produced a pamphlet recording his thoughts on the maritime disaster. These memories took on a strange resonance when his mother passed away on 14 April 1944, the thirty-second anniversary of the tragedy that had taken his father's life. By this time, Jack's two sons were serving their country in the Second World War. The death of one of them, Edward, while on active duty in the Pacific, brought about a terminal bout of depression for Jack Thayer. In September 1945, he drove a car belonging to his wife Lois, parked it near a trolley bus terminus and committed suicide. Shocked employees of the Pennsylvania Trolley Company discovered the body slumped in the front seat. Jack Thayer had brought about his own death by slashing his throat and wrists with a razor.

ANNIE ROBINSON
WOMAN OVERBOARD!

'It is the sort of thing one doesn't like to talk much about afterward.'

When King George V and Queen Mary visited Liverpool to open a new dock in July 1913, the day was marred when a wall collapsed on a landing stage along the royal route. The accident seriously injured two people and killed a man who suffered a broken skull. Their majesties were then reminded of an even greater tragedy when they were introduced to White Line stewardess Annie Robinson, a survivor of the *Titanic*. The royal couple congratulated Mrs Robinson on her fortunate escape and were most interested to hear her story. They asked many questions about the disaster, but found their seafaring subject was extremely reluctant to discuss the calamity other than to agree that 'more lives could have been saved.'

The *Titanic* tragedy was not the first time that Annie Robinson had served on a ship that had struck an iceberg. While working for the Canadian Pacific Line in 1907, she was serving on board the SS *Lake Champlain*, that was carrying 100 passengers from Liverpool to Montreal, when the ship struck an iceberg off Cape Race. With a hole in her bow, the vessel limped to the safety of St John's, Nova Scotia. The forty-two-year-old widow seemed to have got over these two grim experiences when she travelled as a passenger from Liverpool on the Leyland Line vessel *Devonian* in October 1914. Bound for Boston, she planned to visit her daughter and son-in-law, Mr and Mrs James Prentiss. However, on the day before the vessel

Annie Robinson escaped from two ships sunk by icebergs.

was due to reach her final destination, the sea became enveloped in a thick fog. The constant warning sound of the ship's fog horn seemed to unnerve the traumatised passenger who suddenly seemed convinced that there was going to be another disaster. At 10.30 in the evening, she becoming increasingly agitated and was seen running out of the main saloon in a high state of excitement. When she failed to appear for breakfast the next morning, it was discovered that Annie Robinson had committed suicide by leaping overboard to her death.

Boston was also the intended destination for Juha Niskanen when he boarded the *Titanic* at Southampton. After residing in America for three years, he had returned home to his native Finland. Travelling in steerage with his companion Juho Stranden, the two men reached the boat deck and, according to their story, helped with the loading of a lifeboat, then climbed in themselves and were among the fortunate few third-class male passengers that escaped safely from the sinking ship. Fifteen years later, the lure of gold caused Niskanen to move from New England to California. Settling in Cazedero to work a claim, he gradually became a recluse. Depressed over his failure to make his fortune, the fifty-four-year-old drifter set fire to his cabin and committed suicide. Police officers entered the gutted dwelling and discovered the charred body of the crazed prospector with a gunshot shot wound to the head.

Annie Robinson was rescued in the same lifeboat as Jane Quick and her two young daughters, eight-year-old Winifred and two-year-old Phyllis. When met by her husband in Detroit, Jane Quick sobbed 'Oh Fred, it was terrible. I never expected to see my loved ones again.' Fred Quick had emigrated from Plymouth two years earlier and arranged for his family to join him by travelling on the *Titanic*. After first being told that there was only room for the children, the trio squeezed into a lifeboat when Jane Quick insisted: 'Either we go together or not at all.' While eldest daughter Winifred lived to become one of the last survivors of the Titanic, dying aged ninety-eight in 2002, Phyllis killed herself with a gunshot wound to the head in 1954. Aged only forty-five, she was survived by a husband and four children. Another ill-fated resident of Detroit was Welsh-born, John Morgan Davis. At the age of nine, he escaped from the *Titanic* accompanied by his widowed mother Agnes. Nearly forty years later, John was working as a drugstore clerk in Detroit. Recently divorced from his wife Olive, the father of two children used his pharmaceutical knowledge to administer a lethal dose of barbiturate poisoning, prematurely ending his life at the age of forty-eight in December 1951.

Although considered by the world at large to be lucky to be alive, the survivors of the *Titanic* had to live with the harrowing memories of that terrible night. They had to cope with post-traumatic stress disorder without modern-day knowledge that recognises such victims are vulnerable to suicide. Annie Robinson was unable to talk about her horrifying experience even when plied with questions by the monarch: 'It is the sort of thing one doesn't like to talk much about afterward,' she explained, 'It was too terrible.'

BIBLIOGRAPHY & SOURCES

General Sources

Bryceson, Dave. *The Titanic Disaster: As Reported in the British National Press April-July 1912*. Yeovil, Patrick Stephens Ltd, 1997.

Caren, Eric and Goldman, Steve. *Extra Titanic: The Story of the Disaster in the Newspapers of the Day*, USA, Book Sales Inc., 1998

Matthews, H.C.G. and Harris, Brian. Oxford Dictionary of National Biography, Oxford, Oxford University Press, 2004

Website sources:

Ancestry.com: www.ancestry.com

Encyclopedia Titanica: www.encyclopedia-titanica.org

Find My Past: www.findmypast.co.uk

Newsbank: http//:infoweb.newsbank.com

New York Times: www.nytimes.com

Nineteenth Century Newspapers: http://infotrac.galegroup.com

Times Digital Archive:

Titanic Inquiry Project: www.titanic inquiry.org

Wikipedia: www.wikipedia.org

MYSTERY AND CRIME ON THE WHITE STAR LINE

William Murdoch: 'Women and Children First'

Brown, Rustie. *The* Titanic, *the Psychic and the Sea*, Blue Harbor, 1981

Lord, Walter. *The Night Lives On*, Harmondsworth. Penguin Books Ltd., 1986

Daily Sketch, Passenger's Tribute To First Officer Murdoch, 30 April 1912

Daily Sketch, Man Who Was Pulled Back, 4 May 1912

The *Denver Post*, Frantic Men Who Tried to Rush Lifeboats Are Shot Dead, 19 April 1912

New York Herald, Cries of Lost Mingled With Music Of Sinking Band, 19 April 1912

The Times, Mr George Brayton, 20 April 1912

Robert Hichens: Sinking Lower and Lower

Holgate, Mike. *The Man Who Sank the* Titanic, Family History Monthly, March 2010

Whatever Happened to Robert Hichens by Phillip Gowan and Brian Meister, Enclopedia Titanica, [n.d.]

Denver Post, Drunken Sailor Only Man in Mrs Astor's Boat, 19 April 1912

Herald & Express, Man With a Revolver, 13 November 1933

New York Herald, Told to Watch for Ice, Says Man at Wheel, 19 April 1912

Torquay Times & South Devon Advertiser, Alleged Shooting Scene in Torquay, 15 November 1933

William Mintram: Redemption of a Wife Killer

Moloney, Senan. McGough the Killer, Encyclopedia Titanica 2008

The Times, [William Mintram] The Assizes, Western Circuit, 24 November 1902

Western Morning News, [Walter Hurst] Leap of 75 Feet, 29 April 1912

Michel Navratil: The Orphans of the Titanic

Molony, Senan. A Tale of Hoffman, Encyclopedia Titanica 2005

New York Herald, Two Sea Waifs Identified By Scars On Baby's Body, 24 April 1912

New York Times, Michel Navratil, Titanic Survivor, 92, 1 February 2001

George McGough: Manslaughter on the High Seas

Moloney, Senan. McGough the Killer, Encyclopedia Titanica 2008

Barry Dock News, Alleged Murder of A Barry Boarding House Keeper, 13 April 1900

Hampshire Advertiser, Charge of Murder Against A Seaman At Southampton, 28 April 1900

Hampshire Advertiser, Manslaughter On The High Seas, 4 July 1900

New York Times, Priests Consoled The Doomed, 20 April 1912

South Wales Echo, Manslaughter On A Cardiff-Laden Vessel, 3 July 1900

Jay Yates: Gambling With His Life

Cook, Kevin. Titanic *Thompson: The Man Who Bet On Everything*, London, Picador, 2011

Chicago Inter Ocean, Human Buzzards of Sea Sink With *Titanic*, 20 April 1912

Chicago Inter Ocean, Jay Yates, Gambler, One of the Heroes, 21 April 1912
Findlay Courier, The Unsinkable Jay Yates, 17 Jan 1998
Hancock Courier [Arrest of Jay Yates] 13 June 1912
New York Herald, Gamblers Perish with the Titanic, 21 April 1912
Witney Gazette, Gamblers on *Titanic* Escape By Dressing as Women, 11
    May 1912

Charles Barnes: Double Trouble
Holgate, Mike. The Mystery of Charles Barnes and Robert Barnhouse,
    Encyclopedia Titanica 2009
Torquay Directory & South Devon Journal, Claim For Loss on the 'Titanic',
    23 April 1913
Torquay Times & South Devon Advertiser, Echo Of The *Titanic* Disaster: The
    Strange Story Of The Man With Two Names, 25 April 1913

Lorraine Allison: Back From The Dead
Connecticut Post, [Oskar Palmquist],14 April 1998
New York Times, *Titanic* Disaster Survivor Drowns in a Shallow Pond,
    April 19, 1925
Stamford Advocate, Pequonnock River Has a Legacy of Death, 7 December
    2010
San Francisco Examiner, Herman Klaber On Board *Titanic*, 16 April 1912
Chicago Examiner, Titanic Widow Killed By A Former Suitor, 25 February
    1914
Lynch, Don. Marschall, Ken. Whatever Happened To Lorraine Allison?
    in Titanic - *An Illustrated History*, London, Hodder & Stoughton, 1992
Chicago Tribune, Child Feared Lost On *Titanic* Reported Living In Michigan,
    5 September 1940
The Times, [Reprieve of Alice Cleaver], 15 March 1909

Katherine Scott: Double Tragedy
Holgate, Mike. Double Tragedy, *Devon Life*, April 1997
Stocker, Mark. Lady Kathleen Scott, *Oxford Dictionary of National Biography*,
    Oxford, Oxford Press, 2004
King, H.G. Robert Falcon Scott, *Oxford Dictionary of National Biography*,
    Oxford, Oxford Press, 2004
www.telegraph.co.uk. Katherine Scott's Last Letter to Her Husband, 15
    January 2011

Jack Johnson: Fare Thee Well, *Titanic*
Giller, Norman & Duncanson, Neil. *Crown of Thorns*, London, Boxtree Ltd., 1992
Oliver, Paul. *The Story of the Blues*, London, Barrie and Rockliff, 1969

Captain Haddock: Mutiny on the Olympic
Daily Sketch, Olympic Hold-Up, 1 May 1912
Daily Sketch, Guilty - But Let Off, 6 May 1912
The Times, *Olympic* Delayed, 25 April 1912
The Times, Midnight Incident In The Liner, 27 April 1912
The Times, The *Olympic*'s Seamen, 6 May 1912

PROPHETS OF DOOM
Captain Smith: The Last Voyage
McConnell, Anna. Edward John Smith, *Oxford Dictionary of National Biography*, Oxford. Oxford University Press, 2004
Chicago Tribune, Captain Smith Declared To Friends He Would Sink With The Vessel, 18 April 1912
New York Herald, Captain's Smith's Bad Luck Came After 43 Years Unmarred Record, 16 April 1912
New York Times, Captain Smith, 16 April 1912
Gardner, Martin. *The Wreck of the* Titanic *Foretold?*, New York, Prometheus Books 1986

John Jacob Astor: The Judgement of God
Denver Post, Col. Astor's Death On Honeymoon is Shock to Country, 16 April 1912
Denver Post, Judgement of God on Astor Says Pastor Who Denounced Marriage, 18 April 1912
Denver Post, Greatest Astor of Them All, 19 April 1912
New York Times, Son For Mrs Astor; Named For Father, 15 August 1912

Wallace Hartley: Nearer My God To Thee
Lord, Walter. *The Sound of Music from The Night Lives On*, London, Penguin, 1986
Daily Sketch, Nearer, My God, To Thee, 22 April 1912
Daily Sketch, 30,000 Mourners At Burial of *Titanic* Bandmaster, 20 May 1912

Daily Sketch, Titanic's Bandsmen: Impressive Memorial Concert, 25 May 1912

Denver Post, Hymn They Learned At Mother's Knee Rang in Ears of the Dying,18 April 1912

New York Herald, Band Played Nearer, My God, As the Titanic Sank, Cries of Lost Mingling with the Music, 19 April 1912

William Stead: A Message From Beyond the Grave
Boyden, Joseph O., William Thomas Stead, *Oxford Dictionary of National Biography*. Oxford, Oxford University Press 2004

William T Stead and the *Pall Mall Gazette* @ devil.co.uk

Daily Sketch, Psychic Interview With Mr Stead, 14 May 1912

New York Herald, W.T. Stead Had Described His Own Fate In A Story, 18 April 1912

Dr William Minahan: The Gypy's Curse
Chicago Tribune, Shotgun Ends Student's Life: Jilted Theory, 3 February 1923

Chicago Tribune, Third Tragedy in Family, 19 February 1925

Chicago Tribune, Third Suicide in Family Mystery, 20 February 1925

Daily Mail, Saved By A Dream, 18 April 1912

Denver Post, Gypsy Told Doctor He Would Lose His Life in a Sea Disaster, 17 April 1912

Denver Post, Dream Kept Man Off *Titanic*, 18 April 1912

Margaret Brown: Heroine of the Titanic
Molony. Senan. Riddle of the Sphynx, Encyclopedia Titanica 2008

Daily Sketch, Hope Diamond Again!, 23 April 1912

Denver Post, Story of Mrs Brown's Girlhood and Marriage Like Romance, 19 April 1912

New York Times, Women Revealed As Heroines By Wreck, 20 April 1912

Helen Bishop: A Threefold Prophecy
Bangor Daily Commercial, Was The First Woman in Lifeboat, 19 April 1912

Dowagiac Daily News, Mr and Mrs Bishop Give First Authentic Interview Concerning *Titanic* Disaster, 20 April 1912

Dowagiac Daily News, [Death of Helen Bishop and marriage of Dickinson Bishop] 16 March 1916

New York Times, *Titanic* Survivor Dying, 6 November 1913

Edith Russell: Dying in Luxurious Squalor

MacQuilty, William. *Titanic* Memories: The Making of a Night To Remember, London. National Maritime Museum 2001

Randy Bryan Bigham, Edith Louise Rosenbaum Russell (1879-1975), Encyclopedia Titanica, [n.d.]

New York Times, Girl Survivor Has Praise For Ismay, 23 April 1912

Women's Wear Daily, Edith Rosenbaum Reported Hurt in Automobile Accident, 22 August 1911

Major Archibald Butt: The Admirable Crichton

Bangor Daily Commercial, Major Butt Made His Will In Fear of Death, 19 April 1912

Denver Post. Butt An Honour To His Uniform, 19 April 1912

New York Herald, Major Archibald Butt, The Admirable Crichton, 21 April 1912

Henry Forbes Julian: Unlucky Thirteen

Julian, Hester. *Memorials of Henry Forbes Julian*, London, Charles Griffin& Co., 1914

The Times, In Memoriam, 15 April 1913

Torquay Times & South Devon Advertiser, A '*Titanic* Hero', 26 April 1912

Transactions of the Devonshire Association, Henry Forbes Julian, Vol 44, 1912

Nostradamus: The Titanic's Horoscope Horror

Roberts, Henry C. *The Complete Prophecies of Nostradamus*, London, Granada Publishing 1984

Penny Illustrated, The *Titanic* And The 'Stars', 27 April 1912

Daily Sketch, 'Everything Against Us', 22 May 1912

WARTIME EXPERIENCES

Ned Parfett: The *Titanic* Newsboy

New York Herald, The Newspapers' Part In *Titanic* Wreck, 21 April 1912

Penny Illustrated, The *Titanic* Scream, 11 May 1912

The Times, Fate of a *Titanic* Newsboy, 11 November 1998

Titanic Newsboy's Tragic Fate, Your Family History, May 2010

Murphy, Gavin. The Boy in the Picture, Encyclopedia Titanica 2002

John Priest: Jonah of the High Seas

The Times, A Fireman's Adventures

Jessop, Violet. *Titanic Survivor*, New York, Sheridan House 1997

Edith Pears: Wartime Loss and the Victoria Cross

London Gazette, Frank Bernard Wearne VC, 2 August 1917

Lovell, Nicholas. The Five Victoria Crosses of Bromsgrove School, website: Demon.co.uk, 1996

John Hume: The Violinist and the Mutilated Nurse

Hume, Yvonne. *The First Violin*, Stenlake Publishing, Catrine, Ayrshire, 2011

Molony, Senan. *Titanic's* Violinist and a Villainous Murder, Encyclopedia Titanica 2004

The Scotsman, The Dumfries Atrocity Hoax, 29 December 1914.

The Scotsman, The Atrocity Hoax, 30 December 1914.

The Star, A Nurse's Tragedy, 16 September 1914

Charles Lightoller: A Life On The Ocean Wave

Lightoller, Commander. Titanic *and Other Ships*, London, Ivor Nicholson and Watson, 1935

Christian Science Sentinel, Testimonies from the Field, December 1912

New York Times, Obituary: C.H. Lightoller, 78, Officer On Titanic,

The Times, The Destruction of German Submarines: Prize Bounty, 15 July 1919

The Times, Obituary, 9 December 1952

Stenson, Patrick, *Titanic Voyager: The Odyssey of C.H. Lightoller*, Halsgrove, 2011

SOS: STORIES OF SUICIDE

Bruce Ismay: The Coward of the *Titanic*

Gordon-Read, J. Bruce Ismay, *Oxford Dictionary of National Biography*, Oxford, Oxford University Press, 2008

Lord. Walter. *The Night Lives On*, London, Penguin Books, 1987

Mehl, Margaret, Last of the Last: How Masabumi Hosono's Night Was Forgotten, Encyclopedia Titanica, 2003

Daily Sketch, [Bruce Ismay] 'Nothing I Am Sorry For' 22 April 1912

The Guardian, [Masabumi Hosono], 13 December 1997

The Times, [West family] A flask of hot milk for his family– then father went back to his doom on *Titanic*, 26 March 2009

Dr Henry Frauenthal: Prey to Death
The Denver Post, Panic Terrible Just Before Vessel Sank, 19 April 1912
New York Herald, Cripples To Greet Titanic Survivor, 21 April 1912
New York Times, Dr H.W. Frauenthal is Killed by Fall, 12 March 1927
New York Times, Frauenthal Leaves Estate To Hospital, 15 March 1927

George Brereton: Death of a Conman
Herbold, Mike. George A. Brereton - Mystery Man, Encyclopedia Titanica 2001
Lord, Walter. *The Night Lives On*, London, Penguin, 1986
Los Angeles Times, Race Swindler Suspects Held, 5 July 1933
Los Angeles Times, Tragedy Repeats in Dual Suicide, 17 July 1942
New York Herald, Gamblers Perish with the *Titanic*, 21 April 1912
New York Sun, Swindlers at Work in *Titanic* Lifeboats, June 28 1912
New York Times, Reads Bulletin, Collapses, 16 April 1912

Washington Dodge: A Matter of Honour
The Daily Telegraph, Captain's Suicide on the Bridge, 19 April 1912
The Globe and Commercial Advertiser, How the Great *Titanic* Raced To Destruction, 19 April 1912
New York Herald, The *Titanic*'s Captain Shot Himself As The Ship Went Down With Band Playing, 19 April 1912
San Francisco Examiner, Dr Washington Dodge Tries Suicide; May Die, 22 June 1919
San Francisco Examiner, Dr Dodge Is Operated On , 23 June 1919
San Francisco Examiner, Dr Dodge Dies From Wounds He Inflicted, 1 July 1919
Washington Times, Captain Smith Ended Life When Titanic Began To Founder,19 April 1912

Frederick Fleet: Lookout For Danger
Daily Sketch, Lookout Man and the Berg, 9 May 1912
New York Herald, Told to Watch for Ice, Says Man at the Wheel, 19 April 1912
New York Herald, Man In Crow's Nest Tells Of Sighting Ice, 24 April 1912
New York Times, *Titanic* Lookout Is Dead By Hanging After Wife's Death, 12 January 1965.

New York World, Lookout Claims Murdoch Shot Himself, 21 April 1912
Southampton Echo, *Titanic* Survivor Found Hanged, 11 January 1965

Jack Thayer: A Sketchy Memory
Jack Thayer:
Brooklyn Daily Eagle, Jack Thayer's Father Lost In Disaster, 21 April 1912
Philadelphia Inquirer, Obituary: Mrs John Thayer, 15 April 1944
Philadelphia Inquirer, Obituary: Jack Thayer, 23 September 1945
William Lucas:
Daily Sketch, Away Just In Time, 8 May 1912
Syracuse Herald, *Titanic* Survivor Suicide, 13 November 1921
The Times, Man Shot In Train, 22 September 1921

Annie Robinson: Woman Overboard!
Boston Daily Globe, Woman Leaps From *Devonian*, 11 October 1914
Daily Mining Gazette, Obituary: John Morgan Davis, 17 December 1951
Detroit Journal, [Return of Mrs Quick], 20 April 1912
New York Times, King to *Titanic* Survivor, 12 July 1913
New York Times, *Titanic* Survivor Lost, 11 October 1914
Santa Rosa Democrat, Recluse Fires Cabin, Then Kills Self, 14 August 1927
The Times, Royal Review In The Mersey, 12 July 1913